...VIEW

BUSINESS
SCHOOL
COMPANION

Books in The Princeton Review Series

Cracking the ACT
Cracking the ACT with Sample Tests on Computer Disk
Cracking the GED
Cracking the GMAT
Cracking the GMAT with Sample Tests on Computer Disk
Cracking the GRE
Cracking the GRE with Sample Tests on Computer Disk
Cracking the GRE Psychology Subject Test
Cracking the LSAT
Cracking the LSAT with Sample Tests on Computer Disk
Cracking the MCAT
Cracking the MCAT with Sample Tests on Computer Disk
Cracking the SAT and PSAT
Cracking the SAT and PSAT with Sample Tests on Computer Disk
Cracking the SAT II: Biology Subject Test
Cracking the SAT II: Chemistry Subject Test
Cracking the SAT II: English Subject Tests
Cracking the SAT II: French Subject Test
Cracking the SAT II: History Subject Tests
Cracking the SAT II: Math Subject Tests
Cracking the SAT II: Physics Subject Test
Cracking the SAT II: Spanish Subject Test
Cracking the TOEFL with Audiocassette

Culturescope
Culturescope Elementary
Culturescope High School

SAT Math Workout
SAT Verbal Workout

Don't Be a Chump!
How to Survive Without Your Parents' Money
Speak Now!
Trashproof Resumes

Grammar Smart
Math Smart
Reading Smart
Study Smart
Word Smart: Building an Educated Vocabulary
Word Smart II: How to Build a More Educated Vocabulary
Word Smart Executive
Word Smart Genius
Writing Smart

Grammar Smart Junior
Math Smart Junior
Word Smart Junior
Writing Smart Junior

Law School Companion

Student Access Guide to America's Top Internships
Student Access Guide to College Admissions
Student Access Guide to the Best Business Schools
Student Access Guide to the Best Law Schools
Student Access Guide to the Best Medical Schools
Student Access Guide to the Best 309 Colleges
Student Access Guide to Paying for College
Student Access Guide to Visiting College Campuses
Student Access Guide: The Big Book of Colleges
Student Access Guide: The Internship Bible

Also available on cassette from Living Language

Grammar Smart
Word Smart
Word Smart II

THE PRINCETON REVIEW

BUSINESS SCHOOL COMPANION

The Ultimate Guide to Excelling in Business School and Launching Your Career

H.S. HAMADEH
ANDY RICHARD

Random House, Inc.
New York 1995

ISBN 0-679-76463-1

Manufactured in the United States of America on recycled paper.

9 8 7 6 5 4 3 2

First Edition

Acknowledgments

The authors would like to thank everyone who made this book possible including: the team at Random House, John Katzman, our editor Amy Zavatto, and John Bergdahl, Meher Khambata, and Illeny Maaza for the book's design.

We would also like to thank those who provided support throughout the writing of this book, especially Kirsten, Mitch, and Allen.

Contents

CHAPTER 1

Intro to Business School

Just a few years ago, critics were sounding the death knell of the MBA. MBA hiring dropped off suddenly, as Corporate America slashed thousands of the middle-management positions that had been the primary destinations for graduating MBAs. Whereas ten years ago the average MBA could expect to have 3.8 job offers by the time he or she graduated, in 1993 that figure was only one job offer per MBA.[1] Even prestigious business schools like the University of Virginia's Darden School were hit with a 20 percent decline in on-campus recruiting visits from corporations.

Applications to business schools also plummeted, and the number of people registering for the GMAT declined 20 percent from its peak in 1991.

Although the sharp drop in interest from recruiters and prospective students coincided with the general economic recession of the early 1990s, critics pointed out that the MBA's decline was more than a short-term downturn. Many corporations observed that business schools had become irrelevant and outdated, that MBAs lacked people skills, and that B-schools did not give students the abilities they needed to become good managers.

MAKING A COMEBACK

Lately, however, the MBA has been experiencing a dramatic resurgence to a level not seen since the late 1980s. As salaries have increased, so have applications to business schools across the board, making the competition for acceptance into a top-ranked MBA program very stiff.

Companies are once again flocking to B-schools in search of newly minted MBAs, promising attractive salaries and benefits packages. Much of the stepped-up hiring at business schools has come from the growing management consulting industry, which needs scores of new MBAs to fill associate positions. This is good news for graduating MBA students, who can again expect to choose from among multiple job offers.

New Skills

Part of the renewed interest in MBA programs comes from the fact that graduate business education has improved significantly in the last few years. Business schools responded to the criticism in the early 1990s by revamping their MBA programs to meet the demands of students and corporate recruiters. In particular, B-schools have started to teach more "soft skills," with many schools now requiring courses in leadership and communications. Additionally, many B-schools make incoming MBAs participate in Outward Bound-style team exercises to teach them values like cooperation and trust.

Business schools have also tried to make their curricula more practical. Many B-schools have implemented field projects in which students analyze the problems of a real company and make recommendations to the firm's executives. For instance, the University of Michigan's B-school has adopted medical school style "residencies," in which MBA students gain real-world experience working at local corporations.

"Globalization" has also been a prominent theme in the revamped MBA programs. B-schools like Virginia's Darden have incorporated overseas work-study consulting projects into their curricula, while schools like Wharton offer foreign language courses that teach business conversation.

Flight to Quality

An increasing number of prospective students are narrowing their choices and applying only to the very best B-schools, a phenomenon that the business press has called "a flight to quality." A lot of students have decided that only a degree from a top-ranked school is worth the cost of tuition and two years of lost salary. As a result, most of the recent increase in B-school applications has been felt at only the top fifty or so business schools, while other B-schools are seeing small increases or even declines. At Stanford Business School, for example, applications rose to more than 6,000 in 1995, a 32 percent increase from the prior year, while applications rose more than 20 percent at Columbia and Wharton.[2]

B-School Ethics

MBAs have long suffered from an image problem, particularly in the area of business ethics. Movies like *Wall Street* depicting greedy young MBAs certainly haven't helped the B-school image. In addition, a series of ethical scandals involving MBA students or recent B-school graduates have contributed to the mistaken impression of MBAs as lacking in moral virtue. For instance, a couple of years ago a Harvard Business School student rigged the Finance Club's elections to guarantee that he would be elected club president. Harvard nevertheless allowed the student to graduate, amid much criticism from the press.

Business schools have responded by adopting ethics courses in large numbers. Nearly all major MBA programs now require students to take a business ethics course before graduating (although at many schools, like Harvard, the course is ungraded). Students in these courses might be asked to read a case about a business scandal, like the Salomon Brothers Treasury Bond auction scandal, then debate the morality of alternative courses of action. Other B-schools, such as Indiana and Michigan, have implemented public service projects in which MBA students volunteer their time to help needy families. In addition, there is the "ethical dilemma essay" that you'll now find on most B-school applications. This asks applicants to describe an ethical dilemma they have faced and how they resolved it. Whether these efforts will change the perception of MBAs is uncertain, but the teaching of business ethics is certainly a larger part of the B-school experience than it has ever been.

Rising Costs

The cost of a B-school education continues to rise faster than inflation. The annual tuition and fees at many private schools is now approaching $25,000 per year, or $50,000 for a two-year program. When you include two years of lost salary and interest on school loans, the opportunity cost of getting an MBA can reach $200,000.[3] As a result, the decision to quit a job and borrow money to go to B-School is becoming a harder decision for many students to make. In 1994, *The Economist* conducted a cost-benefit analysis of American B-schools and found that some MBA programs offered a *negative* net present value, meaning that graduates actually *lost* money on their B-school investment!

Part-time MBAs

As the cost of pursuing an MBA rises, an increasing number of business school students are pursuing their MBAs in part-time programs. These programs usually offer weekend and evening classes, which allow participants to keep their full-time jobs while they attend business school. Although the schedule can be grueling, many would-be MBAs are finding that a part-time program is the only way they can pursue the benefits of an MBA without incurring the opportunity cost of quitting their job.

So How Much Do MBAs Earn?

MBA starting salaries have increased steadily during the last several years, even increasing slightly during the 1990-91 recession. But statistics show that your starting salary will depend in large part on your business school's ranking. For B-schools overall, the average starting salary was about $42,000 in 1995, increasing about 2.2 percent from the prior year.[4] For the "Top 20" schools, however, first-year pay packages have increased 36 percent in the last two years alone, recently averaging $87,024 thanks largely to the boom in management consulting.[5]

The starting salaries for B-school graduates with technical backgrounds (like engineering) continue to surpass those with nontechnical backgrounds. In 1995, the average starting salary for MBAs with technical undergraduate degrees was $43,368 versus $39,035 for those with nontechnical degrees.[6]

Finally, your starting salary will depend heavily on how much work experience you had before coming to B-school. Nontechnical MBAs without prior work experience earn on average $38,792 versus $44,811 for those with one to two years of experience, and $54,255 for those with two to four years of experience.[7] Technical MBAs with prior work experience are the ones who really clean up in the job sweepstakes: they earn an average of $50,878 with one to two years of prior work experience, and $60,989 with four years of experience.[8]

The Princeton Review Survey

The Princeton Review has surveyed 15,500 current MBA students and hundreds of admissions officers, recruiters, and business school grads to get the inside story on B-school life and the MBA job market. We include quotes from our surveys throughout the book to give you a realistic look at the B-school experience.

END NOTES

1. *U.S. News & World Report*, March 22, 1993.

2. *Orange County Register*, August 16, 1995.

3. "Interest in MBAs Soars Despite Saturation Fears," *Cincinnati Enquirer*, July 23, 1995.

4. *Id.*

5. *Business Week*, October 24, 1994.

6. "Interest in MBAs Soars Despite Saturation Fears," *Cincinnati Enquirer*, July 23, 1995.

7. *National Association of Colleges and Employers*, 1994 Salary Survey.

8. Id.

CHAPTER 2

Before You Arrive

Your business school experience will be more productive and more enjoyable if you come prepared. Therefore, it's best to think about issues like housing and computer hardware before you arrive for your first day of classes.

HOUSING

Like many graduate students, business school students usually have a choice to live either on- or off-campus. While the breadth of the choices will vary depending on the location and housing situation of the particular school, there are positives and negatives to each alternative that should be considered before making a final decision.

If a school has on-campus living accommodations, the primary benefit in choosing this option is convenience. It is nice to be able to walk to class no matter what the weather is or how tired you are. Also, it makes it easy to go back and forth from school to home in the middle of the day, for example, to eat lunch or change for an interview. Group meetings corporate presentations, and other campus events are also easily accessible, and often there are many MBA students living in the same building, making social relationships easier to form.

On the other hand, sometimes people like to get away from school at night, particularly since business school is such an intense experience. Also, in many cases, the quality of on-campus housing is not as good as what you might find elsewhere, and there is no guarantee that the price will be lower, either.

For these reasons, many students choose to live off-campus in an apartment or rented house. This allows much more leeway in the choice of accommodations; different students can choose different sizes and luxury levels, depending on their price range. It also allows small groups of friends to share a house and spend more social time together. If you're like most MBAs, you've been out of school for a few years and are probably used to living in an apartment; as a result, you may not be ready to live in a dorm or dorm-like atmosphere. By and large, MBA students seem to prefer the flexibility of off-campus accommodations to the convenience of on-campus housing.

Keep in mind, however, that commuting to and from campus can be tiresome, particularly during bad weather. The cost of commuting, either by car or by public transportation, must be factored into a student budget. Off-campus living also makes multiple trips to school impractical, and takes a chunk of time out of your day that could be otherwise productive. Although most students choose to live off-campus, each person must consider her own preferences and the complete set of options available before making a decision.

COMPUTER HARDWARE

In business school, as in business, the personal computer is a very important part of a productive experience. If you don't know how to use a computer when you start B-school, you should at least get comfortable sitting in front of one, because one way or another you're going to spend countless hours with the glare of a computer screen in your face. In addition, many business schools now require incoming students to certify that they have basic computer skills or take a crash course in computing before arriving at B-school. As a result, MBAs leave B-school with an advantage over non-MBAs in terms of computer skills. One Columbia MBA reported that students "are exceptionally computer literate due to the computer initiative requiring each person to own a laptop and use course material provided on the computer network."

Here is an introductory guide to the questions you need to consider regarding computer hardware:

Do I Need to Have My Own Computer?

Technically, no. Most B-schools will have computers available free of charge for student use, and these computers usually have the software and printing capabilities that you will need to complete all your assignments. Also, most of your friends will probably have computers, and they will usually be happy to let you use them. If you're willing to plan ahead and don't mind doing a lot of your school work away from home, then you don't absolutely need your own system.

Practically speaking, however, it becomes quite inconvenient to do everything you want to do without your own computer. Campus computer labs are frequently crowded, and you may have to wait in line for an available machine. If you need to work late at night, it may be difficult to get to and from the machine you need to use. The time it takes in transportation can subtract from an already-crowded schedule. Moreover, computer labs often close at night, so you can find your schedule being dictated by the lab's hours of operation.

Another issue to consider is that it can be next to impossible to save all your work reliably on floppy disks. Furthermore, you may have to sacrifice privacy if you want to work on cover letters or other correspondence. In reality, almost everyone at B-school has his own system and couldn't imagine getting by without it. The best advice we can offer is to make the investment and buy or lease your own personal computer. It's worth it.

Can I Use the Computer I Have Now?

If you have recently purchased a new computer system, your system is probably adequate. However, most MBA students haven't bought a new computer since college, and these machines are probably out-of-date and not powerful enough to serve a business-school student's needs.

What Kind of System Should I Get?

If you do decide to purchase your own computer, or upgrade your existing system, you need to consider carefully the type of system you will want to have at business school. Many schools have standardized their computer systems, and they expect all students to have access to the same type of hardware. In this case, your choice is easy: ask your school's administrative office, and they should be able to tell you exactly which components to look for.

Otherwise, the most important choice you have to make is the type of system you want—Apple- or IBM-compatible. Check with your school to see if all software required for your classes is available for both types of machine. For example, many business programs are available only for IBMs, and these limitations may help determine your purchase.

If there are no constraining factors, then you must decide between the two, and there are good arguments for each choice. Apple computers are highly regarded for their physical design, their graphical capabilities, and their reliability and ease of use in both hardware and systems software; also, with popular software programs or with the new Power PC chip, Apples can usually read IBM-compatible files. On the other hand, Apples do not run as many business software applications and tend to be more expensive than IBM systems. In contrast, IBM-compatibles are reasonably priced, have an amazing array of software, and are used widely in the business world.

In short, if you are used to using an Apple computer and are unfamiliar with an IBM, purchasing an Apple along with software or a chip that reads IBM files, you should get along fine. Otherwise, an IBM-compatible PC is a safer bet, if only because most other MBA students use them and because most software for B-school assignments runs on IBM systems.

Should I Get a Portable or a Desktop PC?

Portable computers, or "laptops," provide mobility and convenience, since you can take them with you to group meetings or work on them at school. Many students value this flexibility and wouldn't think of having a desktop.

There are trade-offs, however. First, laptops can be very pricey, especially if you prefer a color monitor. A color laptop computer can easily cost 25-50 percent more than a desktop with equal capabilities. Furthermore, laptops are not as comfortable to use; their small screens, compressed keyboards, and makeshift mice tend to get tiresome after extended use.

The most important factors to consider in making this decision should be whether you intend to do most of your studying on campus or at home, and whether your MBA program includes lots of team projects, which will require team meetings at various locations. If this describes your scenario, a portable computer would be an excellent investment, especially if you will be completing a large number of assignments in teams.

Do I Need My Own Laser Printer?

Again, the answer to this question is no, but your life will be a lot easier if you have one. Your business school should have community laser printers available for a small per-page charge (in the 10-25 cent range), and if you are very patient you can get by relying on these machines. But with all the papers, spreadsheets, and cover letters that you're going to be writing, it grows very tiresome and time-consuming to have to print out all of your work at school. Also, if you spot an error when you've returned home, you have to go back to campus to print a corrected version. There is also little room for error.

In practice, almost all students who have computers also own their own laser printers. Even if you already own a dot-matrix or ink-jet printer, it pays to upgrade to a laser printer. Some students share the cost of a printer with their roommates, a good idea if you are confident that you can work out ownership issues when eventually you part ways. Another way to save money is to sacrifice a little on print quality. Although many people say that 600 dpi (dots per inch) is required for business correspondence, 300 dpi looks nearly as good and will be fine for virtually everything except your resumes. However, ink-jet printers are generally not worth the small savings in purchase price because their print quality, although good, is not enough for business school projects or correspondence with employers.

What Other Accessories Should I Have?

Nearly every MBA student has a modem, which allows you to send and receive faxes and access e-mail and other information services. Many business schools are moving toward increasing use of on-line based communications with students, and many assignments and class notes are now available through e-mail. In addition, many business schools conduct their entire on-campus recruiting system, including interview sign-ups, solely through an electronic system that can be accessed through a modem. Since modems are generally inexpensive, their purchase is worthwhile for an MBA student if one is not included with your computer.

Although CD-ROM drives may be the wave of the future (and pretty cool, too), they serve very little purpose for the business school student and are an unnecessary investment if you're on a budget.

When and Where Should I Buy My System?

If you have not yet started business school, you should be in no hurry to purchase your computer. Prices of computer hardware tend to go down over time, and waiting even a couple of months can mean significant savings. You should probably purchase your system about a month or two before school starts, to allow for shipping time and give you a chance to familiarize yourself with its features and software.

Most universities also sell computer systems (usually through the campus bookstore) and claim that they offer the best prices available. Many times this claim is true. In reality, however, the savings you can obtain by purchasing through your university are usually very small; the industry has become so competitive that large chain retailers will usually offer comparable prices. In addition, mail-order catalogs (such as MacWarehouse, Microwarehouse, or J&R Sound) offer some of the lowest prices around and often have the added benefit of avoiding sales tax. Furthermore, because students all tend to order computers at the beginning of the school year, your order may not be filled quickly if you plan to buy at school. Before you get to B-school, compare your school's prices to the prices at a local retailer or mail-order catalog. In the absence of substantial savings, you should purchase your computer from another source before arriving at school so you have some time to set up your system and get comfortable using it.

COMPUTER SOFTWARE

When you buy a new computer, you may be tempted to load it up with all the business software in the world. Although there are a few programs that you can safely buy ahead of time, be aware that many of your courses will require specific programs, and there is no sense trying to predict what you are going to need. Also, your school may require the use of certain brands or versions of programs, so you should check before making any sort of investment.

If you have not yet started business school, you should defer your software investment as long as possible. Developers will update programs every year or so, and you should try to get the most recent version available. Unlike hardware, however, software is much less expensive when purchased through school. Universities get an educational discount from software makers, who like to try to win loyalty from young users by offering their products at low prices. As a result, you can often get close to a 50 percent discount if you buy from your bookstore. *Under no circumstances* should you go to a retailer for software of any kind.

Basically, there are four types of software you should have at business school: a word processor (such as Word or WordPerfect); a spreadsheet (such as Excel); a modem communications program; and a presentation package (such as Power Point). The word processor and spreadsheet are absolute necessities in business school and you cannot survive without them. The communications program (which may be available free of charge at school) allows your modem to talk to other computers and send and receive computer files through your phone line. If you buy one, get one with fax capability. The presentation package, while not required, will help with the business school presentations you will surely be making, and it will be particularly advantageous once you start your career.

There will no doubt be other programs that you will be required to use in the course of your graduate education, such as a statistics or accounting program. These programs will be assigned by your professors and made available through school, so there is no sense spending money before you know which program you're supposed to get.

SKILLS

Most business schools expect their students to arrive at B-school already possessing the basic quantitative skills that every MBA student will need. "It helps if you were quantitative before coming to this program," advised one Wharton MBA in our survey. If you were a business or economics major, you should already possess these skills and are probably ready to start business school. On the average, however, only about half of all MBA students enter business school with a business or economics degree. Therefore, there are a lot of liberal arts majors who go to business school these days. If you're one of them, you should consider brushing up on the following skills that you will be expected to have before arriving at school.

Spreadsheets

Most liberal arts majors may not have had much, if any, exposure to using spreadsheet computer programs (such as Lotus or Excel) before going to business school. However, an MBA student probably uses a spreadsheet program more than another type of computer software. Starting business school with some comfort with the use of spreadsheets will therefore be essential. The cheapest way to learn to use a spreadsheet is simply to install spreadsheet software on your computer (you'll need to buy the software eventually anyway) before you start business school, browse the software's manual, and practice doing some simple functions for a few weeks before school begins. Despite their intimidation factor, spreadsheets are much easier to use than you might think, and a few weeks of playing around with one is about all you will need to prepare for business school.

Calculus

Many business schools require their incoming students to certify that they have an understanding of college-level math, usually calculus, before arriving at business school. A college calculus course will normally satisfy this requirement. If an admitted student has not had such a course, she usually must promise to take such a course during the weeks before business school classes begin or, alternatively, register for such a course upon arriving at business school. Even those who have taken calculus may need to review, since some MBA programs require all their incoming students to pass a basic calculus exam before they will be allowed to register for classes. In short, quantitative analysis is the backbone of any MBA program, and business schools take these skills very seriously. If your math skills are weak, you should talk to your school in advance to see what the school requires in terms of math or calculus knowledge before you start school.

Statistics, Accounting, and Economics

Business school professors will expect that most students have had a basic undergraduate course in statistics, accounting, and economics. If you avoided such courses in college, you will have to learn the main concepts of these subjects somehow, either before you arrive at school or as soon as you get there. Chapters 8, 11, and 12 of this book contain some of the key concepts in these courses and can serve as an abbreviated review. For a more in-depth treatment, however, you may need to take a review course.

Fortunately, many business schools now offer crash courses in computers, statistics, economics, and accounting for liberal arts majors. These review courses are usually designed for beginners and are intended to put business-majors and liberal-arts-majors on an even footing when classes begin. If you need such a review, find out from your school whether review courses will be offered either before regular classes begin or in the first weeks of the semester. If so, you can wait and do your review when you get to business school.

CHAPTER 3

MBA Social Life

While the types of people who attend any business school will vary depending on the size, location, and nature of the particular program, there are a few things that can be said about the social life at just about any school. Because business is inherently a people-oriented activity and requires good social skills for success, most MBA students are outgoing and enjoy meeting new people. "Student interaction is frequent and strong," confirmed one University of Florida MBA. "Everyone is very friendly." Also, most students realize that at least some of the value of their degree will come to fruition in the relationships that they form for business contacts down the road. As a result, you can be sure to have opportunities to meet new people in business school and form a number of lasting friendships. One Berkeley MBA student in our survey reported that the school has a "splendid social life," while a Cornell MBA commented that "we are all each other's support networks and it's wonderful." On the other hand, a Texas-Arlington MBA complained that "there are more geeks here than at any other school in America."

Business schools are widely known among the public for being rather homogeneous. The fact is, MBA programs usually attract a much more diverse group of students than undergraduate colleges do. Furthermore, because MBA programs are typically small, there is necessarily much more interaction between different ethnic and social groups. This creates an atmosphere of openness to difference that facilitates the development of social bonds.

The diversity at business schools is different from the widely held notion of diversity on college campuses. The most obvious difference among business school students is the variety of ages of people who attend. Although it is rare to see anyone right out of undergraduate school, many students are only one or two years out of college. By the same token, a good percentage of the students at most MBA programs are over the age of thirty. Many have families and have been in the work force for ten years or more. This diversity helps everybody learn to communicate with people of various ages. At the same time, it can be frustrating for people because many of their classmates have completely different social goals. While some of the younger people may be excited to form new social relationships, many of the older ones are content with their private lives and may not be looking to invest as much in friendships. On the other hand, many students who have been working for a few more years may find some of the social behavior of the younger people a bit immature and at times exclusionary.

Another source of diversity is the international component of many student bodies. Particularly at some of the more prestigious programs, people come from all over the world to study at American business schools. This too is a great source of new insights and perspectives, not only on business issues but also for social opportunities. A Washington University MBA said the school "encourages American students to form groups with and act as a support to foreign students." While most Americans are very helpful and hospitable to people from all nations, some international students, particularly the less outgoing ones, may sense that they do not feel truly comfortable in an American social environment. This is partly because of language difficulties and partly because of the inevitable cultural adjustments that come with living in a foreign country.

Whatever the case, though, business school is a socially intense environment that is a breeding ground for new and lasting friendships. Because of the small size of the community, the heavy workload, and the generally outgoing nature of the students, by the end of the program most people know just about everyone in their class. Furthermore, most people naturally develop solid friendships that will last well beyond graduation. These relationships take root in social situations, in the course of school work, or through extra-curricular activities; they also develop through the course of the job search, where many people look for similar types of positions.

MBA students also like to throw parties. Whether it be an individual student, a group of housemates, or a school organization, there will be no shortage of opportunities to meet other people in an informal setting. "We certainly party," wrote one Wyoming MBA. Part of the reason why many people go back to school is to get a final taste of life as a student, and they don't waste the opportunity to enjoy their freedom. "For those who like to party," reported one University of Chicago MBA, "there are plenty of events at least three nights a week. I really feel like I'm back in college!" And, of course, people like to let off steam by drinking once in a while. "Kegs every Friday at 5:30!" commented one happy Duke MBA. There is usually no shortage of alcoholic consumption in business school.

In many ways, the sense of community at B-school makes people behave in a more mature way, because they know that they have to live with their classmates for a good deal of time; they also want to keep a good reputation for potential future business dealings. There are very few secrets within a class; people like to talk, and word travels fast. A good rule of thumb in business school is not to do anything you wouldn't do if you were running for political office.

And, of course, there is the subject of dating. Inevitably, romantic relationships do sprout due to the intensive nature of an MBA program and the close interaction among classmates. However, people who profess to be looking for a "mate" at business school often become frustrated quickly by the perceived lack of opportunity. "There is no such thing as dating at HBS," complained one Harvard MBA in our survey. One problem is that many students are either married or have significant others who live with them. Wrote a Virginia MBA: "Darden is great for married students...[but] the workload limits the social scene for singles." Furthermore, most business-school populations are about 75 percent male, making the numbers difficult to work out for everyone. And finally, people are often gun-shy about dating someone in their class because of potential social ramifications, particularly if things go sour. In short, while romantic relationships do develop, the intensity of B-school and the varying stages of life its students are in, puts finding a love interest on the bottom of the priority list for many MBA students.

CHAPTER 4

Academics:
What to Expect

A primary reason why students go to business school is to gain the skills, concepts, and intellectual tools needed to perform more effectively in the business world. Since most of your time at business school will be spent either in the classroom or working on homework assignments and group projects, your academic experience will largely shape your overall business school experience.

MBA SUMMER CAMP

The first year of B-school usually begins with a pre-term, also known as "MBA Summer Camp," which may be several days to several weeks in length. At pre-term, incoming MBA students receive "brush-up" review courses in accounting, statistics, basic math or calculus, and economics. A course in basic computer skills may also be included. The main point of pre-term is to place incoming students on a more or less "equal" footing, so former sociology majors will have some of the quantitative skills that business majors have.

Of course, a big part of pre-term is the socializing and bonding that occurs among classmates. The "cliques" that form at pre-term usually endure through graduation, and students who miss pre-term report feeling "left out" for most of the first semester of B-school. Often, the teams in which students will complete their first-year assignments are formed at pre-term, so students may spend this time keeping a look out for potential teammates.

Some MBA schools cap off pre-term with an Outward Bound type experience, in which student teams complete various physical and mental tasks, such as puzzle games or rock climbing. These "team building" exercises are a recent fad in business schools, and although many students say that the value of such exercises is minimal, business schools claim that the experience builds team cooperation and prepares students for the year to come.

THE FIRST-YEAR CURRICULUM

Upon arrival, the incoming first year class is usually divided into sections or "cohorts" of fifty to seventy students. The students in a cohort take classes together, host cohort parties, and become a "school within a school," with cohort friendships lasting throughout B-school and beyond. "Section life is a great experience. You develop great camaraderie with classmates from diverse cultural and professional backgrounds," noted one Harvard MBA.

The workload in the first year of business school generally ranges from "moderately heavy" to "brutal." Business schools like to cram the basic business courses into the first year of the program, and when you include job searches, clubs, and social events, your time soon becomes your most scarce resource. "I worked harder than I've ever worked in my life," moaned one Dartmouth MBA. Even in less rigorous MBA programs, you should expect your first year of B-school to be intense, with the occasional all-nighter working on team projects.

The required series of first-year courses, or "core curriculum," is essentially the same at most B-schools. First year MBAs are generally required to take introductory courses in marketing, finance, statistics, economics, accounting, and operations management. Students with a background in one or more of these areas are often permitted to waive the course, by passing a waiver exam or presenting credentials, and substitute an elective course in its place. For most students, however, elective courses will not begin until the second year of the program.

The first year curriculum may also include a course in leadership or communications skills in which students discuss softer workplace issues, such as diversity and quality of life. Such courses are a relatively recent phenomenon at business schools and have been implemented in response to the criticism that while MBAs graduate with excellent quantitative skills, they lack many of the softer skills required of an effective manager. A first-year leadership course may also require students to complete evaluations of themselves and their teammates, sometimes with the aid of a scored personality test. On the whole, MBAs have tended to be critical of such courses, calling them "touchy-feely" and a "waste of time," and give the courses low points on course evaluations.

Finally, the core curriculum may also include a field project, in cooperation with a local business, in which student teams analyze a discrete issue facing the company and present formal recommendations. The field project is designed to give you real world experience and a chance to apply what you're learning in class to an actual business problem.

THE CLASSROOM EXPERIENCE

Part of what makes business school so different from college is that in B-school much of your learning will come from other students. Therefore, class discussions are a big part of the B-school experience. "We have terrific and lively class discussion," reports one Virginia MBA. "Classes are routinely interrupted with laughter and applause."

Even the classroom environment is designed to encourage participation and foster debate. Students are often seated in ampitheatre-like classrooms, more intimate in size than a typical college lecture hall. Students usually display "name tents" (or cardboard placards bearing their name) on their desks. Professors open discussions on a case or reading assignment by asking for volunteers or cold-calling students by referring to their name tents. B-schools further encourage discussions by assigning a portion of the grade based on class participation, although this grading system encourages some students to offer frequent and irrelevant comments in the hope of accumulating participation points. "Teachers place such emphasis on class participation, people talk just to hear themselves speak," complained a University of Iowa MBA.

The teaching quality at B-schools tends to be uneven and has been a major gripe of many MBAs. The majority of students polled felt that their professors tend to be either very good or egregiously bad. "It's hit or miss with the quality of teaching," reported one

Claremont MBA. "Profs are either great or disappointing. No in-between." Wrote a University of Colorado MBA: "Some professors are fantastic. Others are barely tolerable!"

STUDY SUGGESTIONS

Business school is very demanding, so it is important to be efficient with your time and energy. Even the most talented students can have difficulty getting everything they want out of their MBA program without an organized, well-balanced plan of attack. With this in mind, here are a few general suggestions to help you make your academic experience as rewarding as possible.

Prioritize

Set your priorities and stick to them. It's impossible to take advantage of everything your school has to offer. Between academics, extra-curricular activities, and the job search, you could pass on sleep for weeks and still not do all the things you want. "It moves so fast, there's no time to fall behind. Good time management skills are essential," a Duke MBA advised. Just like in the business world, there is an opportunity cost to every choice you make, and you need to focus on what is important to you and say no to the rest.

Therefore, it is crucial that you set your priorities and plan your time accordingly. Is a stellar transcript your ultimate goal? Then focus on your schoolwork. Are leadership activities your bread and butter? Then get involved. Is an exciting first job in an unconventional field your dream? Then work hard at networking. But keep in mind that everyone else in your class is about as capable and motivated as you are, and it is impossible to do everything effectively. One Indiana University MBA said the trick is to learn how to "master balancing the demands of the program and your social life, so that you can enjoy your experience immensely." Choose a few goals that you want to reach and stick to them; let everything else take a back seat.

Form a Study Group

Some business schools assign their students to study groups, while others leave the decision up to you. In either case, study groups can be an excellent way to spread out some of the workload and use your time more efficiently. If reading assignments during a particular week are especially heavy, you could split up the assignments and have each group member summarize his part for the others. Or when final exam time rolls around, your fellow students may have class notes, or an understanding of certain concepts, that you missed during the semester. Another benefit of forming a study group is that your fellow group members can become some of your best friends at school. However you use them, study groups can take a lot of pressure off the individual student by spreading out the work.

At the same time, you must not rely on your study group for everything. When you don't read a case, no matter how well your study group summarizes it for you, you will not get as much out of the case or class discussion as the person who reads it for himself. In addition, it can be difficult to coordinate group members' schedules and find a convenient meeting place and time. Making such arrangements can sometimes become as time-consuming as the studying itself.

If you recognize its limitations and plan accordingly, however, the study group can be an invaluable source of assistance and support throughout your academic experience at business school.

Get Help

Take advantage of office hours with both teaching assistants and professors. Office hours are a great way to explore areas in which you have a particular interest, to get to know the faculty, or to gain a better understanding of subjects or assignments with which you may be having difficulty. Business school professors are generally very accessible and open to student interaction, and TAs would sit around doing nothing if it weren't for curious MBA students. "Professors are helpful and friendly. They don't act superior or intimidating," wrote one University of Alabama MBA. A Cornell MBA wrote that "the professors' open-door policy is a big plus. It's not uncommon for professors to give out their home phone number, take students on a field trip, or have them over for dinner." If you take advantage of these resources, you can gain that little extra insight that you wouldn't have access to otherwise.

Attend Review Sessions

Much of the learning in your courses will take place at optional review sessions. Although professors are generally not supposed to present new information during review sessions, they often do, so it's important to attend. "The review sessions cram information down your throat. You don't learn—you survive!" a Notre Dame MBA exclaimed.

Be Observant

Take the time to understand your courses and your professors. The best thing you can do to use your study time effectively is to understand how your professors think and how they view the subject matters they are teaching. Spend the first few class sessions observing such things as lecture styles and how professors integrate assigned readings into lectures and discussions. After a few class sessions, you should be able to get a feel for how each course will be conducted. Once you get a feel for the important issues, you should spend your study hours working toward meeting the professor's objectives.

Differences in the styles of classes can be reflected in several ways. You may find that for one professor, cases are the most important materials in the course and other readings are assigned simply for background information, referred to only briefly, if at all, during class discussion. In another prof's class, the lectures may be interesting, but the real meat of the course is in the textbook. For yet another, cases and lectures are largely insignificant and the only thing that counts is being able to solve the assigned problems.

Even two professors teaching the exact same course can vary widely in their approaches. For example, one marketing professor might enjoy the quantitative side of the assigned cases, and focus on numerical analysis in class discussion. At the same time, another might place more importance on the strategic implications of marketing decisions or on the creative aspect of marketing campaigns. Often, these preferences are reflected in grading, assignments, and exams. Once you get a sense of what is important to each individual professor, you can get a lot more out of your study time by focusing on those areas.

GRADES

MBA programs are naturally filled with high achievers. As a result, the competition for good grades is generally intense at the start of business school, as new students see high marks as one more way to stand out among their peers. "The Business School is becoming more and more cut throat. The students are too competitive and the teachers encourage it," moaned one University of Kansas MBA. "Emphasis on grades is somewhat excessive," a Northwestern student complained. It is important to realize, however, that grades have far less importance in business school than they did in college. Before diving blindly into the B-school grade competition, ask yourself what you want to get out of business school and whether top grades fit into your plans.

If you think that good business school grades will give you a significant edge in the job hunt, think again. At this stage, most employers couldn't care less what your B-school grades are. In fact, many schools now discourage or even prohibit students from disclosing their grades to recruiters. In turn, few MBA recruiters ask about grades during interviews, instead preferring to focus their attention on your work experience and professional accomplishments. Many MBAs who graduated at the top of their class report that they achieved their grades at "too great a cost," missing out on social events and networking that prove far more valuable in the long run.

Therefore, unless you're aiming for a job at a firm like McKinsey or Goldman Sachs, which may use grades in their hiring criteria, take the B-school grade competition in moderation. Make sure that your academic intensity isn't causing you to miss out on all of the other things that business school has to offer.

THE SECOND YEAR CURRICULUM

The second year of the MBA program is significantly less intense than the first year. For starters, students usually take fewer courses than they did in the first year. Says a Northwestern MBA, "It can be as challenging as you want it to be. I took several five-course loads and am now planning to take only three just to enjoy life." Moreover, you can take elective courses in your second year, or work on a major, so your courses tend to be more suited to your interests. "The quality of courses increases as you get into your concentration," noted one UConn MBA.

For most MBAs, however, the focus of the second year is on the MBA job search. As early as September of the second year, companies begin coming to campus to make presentations, with job interviews starting as early as October or November. As a result, almost as soon as you return from your summer internship, it's time to polish your resume, press your suit, and begin the job hunt once again. As the recruiting season wears on, second years begin to obsess on the job search, and second year classes contain many empty seats as students miss classes to go on interviews. Whereas the talk in the hallways during first year was on school work or B-school romances, the discussions in second year tend to focus on firms, interviews, and job offers.

Your MBA program may also require a second year thesis as part of your major. The thesis is often written under the supervision of a faculty advisor. Your school may also require a year-long field project in the second year if this was not part of the first year curriculum.

CHAPTER 5

Team Projects

One of the most important skills you will develop in business school is your ability to work as a member of a group. In B-school, "you either like to work in teams or you learn to," one University of North Carolina MBA noted. Employers report that their most successful managers are not those who have the best analytical skills, but those who can be an effective part of a team made up of many different personalities and talents. As a result, business schools have responded by trying to integrate group work into their core curricula to make sure that graduates enter the business world with a good foundation of team skills. Although quantitative analysis is still very important, many people argue that interpersonal skills are what really differentiate the stars in business from the laggards. As a result, much of the academic work in business school is usually done in teams of five or six students.

Unfortunately, working with others is never as easy as we think it should be. "The teamwork thing gets tiresome," confirms one MBA. People have different expectations and capabilities, as well as egos, and intra-team conflict can quickly arouse emotions and ruin an otherwise productive learning experience. "UConn enforces group projects. It's overdone and takes time away from studying," wrote another team-weary B-school student.

COLLABORATING

Here is a set of guidelines to help you make your team projects as enriching as possible.

Choose Carefully

When selecting a team, think carefully about the types of people you want to work with. In some courses, you may be assigned to a team and will have no choice about whom you work with. When you do have a choice, however, consider the different approaches to team formation. For example, some students like to work with people with similar social interests. This can be a big plus because it sets up a relaxed environment and helps you enjoy yourself while you work. But be careful of the potential pitfalls of this strategy. Even if you like a classmate, you may not work well with her, and conflict over schoolwork can threaten your relationship. In addition, if you work only with people who are similar to you, you may not challenge yourself enough to improve your team skills. In the business world, you can't always choose your colleagues, and they won't always be your friends.

On the other end of the spectrum, some students like to work on teams with as much diversity as possible. They purposely seek teammates who differ from them as much as possible in both work experience and cultural orientation. For instance, some American MBA students seek out international students to join their teams in the belief that this provides them with a valuable perspective to business problems. Diversity can indeed help a team by providing a variety of perspectives, and the more types of people with whom you can work, the more prepared you will be to fit into an organizational environment. However, working on a diverse team is not without its challenges. Cultural and language differences can make open communication difficult, and in a time crunch it is crucial that team members understand each other. Also, a group without common interests may have a difficult time maintaining a comfortable work environment over the course of a semester.

When forming a team, determine what you want to get out of your team experience before you select your partners. Most importantly, be prepared for the potential challenges in any group experience and realize that these challenges will exist in the corporate world.

Be Realistic

Set achievable expectations for yourself and your team. It is tempting to envision yourself as a completely selfless team member, willing to devote hours of toil to any project merely for the satisfaction of contributing to the group. It is even more tempting to expect your teammates to be this way. Unfortunately, very few teams are lucky enough to make this vision a reality. The fact of the matter is that people have different time commitments, different objectives, different interests, and different capabilities. Some students are very serious about their coursework; they invest a lot of energy into performing well in class, and they expect their teammates to do the same. Other students are more interested in extracurricular activities and view homework as a necessary evil. Still others are at business school for the sole purpose of landing a higher-paying job and try to get through their B-school education with as little effort as possible.

None of these outlooks is necessarily better or worse than the others. What is important is that you be honest about what you want not just with others, but with yourself. Whether you're shooting for high academic honors or planning on spending the weekends rock climbing, don't try to pretend that you want the same things your teammates want. Be open about your goals, get your group to do the same, and try to plan accordingly in the early stages of your team. Only with a firm understanding of your team's abilities and outside commitments will you be able to reach your potential.

Don't Hold Back

Talk about problems or difficulties before they become insurmountable. Every team is bound to have conflicts. No matter how well you work together, it is more likely than not that there are issues lurking below the surface that could turn into real problems if they are not addressed. For instance, if you feel that your group expects you to devote too much time to what you consider to be unimportant homework assignments, make sure you tell them as soon as possible. Without a clear communication of your feelings, you set up a situation in which you will continue to become angry and your teammates will continue to be disappointed in your contribution. It is much easier to address a complaint before it develops into personal anger and resentment.

Learn from Experience

Experiment with different team designs and pick the one that works best for you. The most important goal of your team will be to complete your projects on time and as well as you want to. In order to do this, you will need to design a process by which you can complete your work in the most efficient manner. Business school students have found that three team designs are the most effective for the academic setting. Following is an overview of how they work and the advantages and disadvantages of each:

One project, one team member.

Many groups like to make one person responsible for each project's completion. This designated project leader oversees the entire process, making all of the major decisions, coordinating and delegating tasks, and tapping the group's resources as she sees fit. Usually, however, this structure means that the project leader does most of the work. Presumably, there will be enough projects during the life of the group for the workload to even out.

In this form of team, projects are often assigned based on the skills of the group members. For example, if one case write-up or team project requires a substantial amount of quantitative work, the person with the best math skills may want to take charge; if another project involves a great deal of written analysis, it may make sense to make the former English major the project leader.

Alternatively, some groups like to do the opposite and allow team members to develop their weaknesses by being responsible for projects in which they may not have expertise. For instance, the former advertising account executive may ask to head the corporate finance assignment. This is an excellent idea, but it may not always be realistic given the severe time pressures in business school. Before your group considers any role reversal, make sure there's enough time available to accompany the learning process.

On balance, this structure is probably the most time-efficient way to complete your course work. It cuts down on bureaucracy and groupthink, enabling swift decision-making and productive use of time. It also allows students to focus on their interests or developmental needs. Finally, it can potentially increase the quality of work because the project has one "visionary" instead of a number of different contributors. You should be aware, however, that there is some risk in allowing one person most of the responsibility for a project. The group does not benefit from the input of all its members, and important perspectives or ideas may be overlooked. More importantly, the members of the group not participating in a particular assignment will miss much of the learning that goes with the assignment's completion, and this becomes particularly apparent at final exam time.

One project, all team members.
Some groups like to get all team members involved in every project. The group will meet for a preliminary assessment of the problem and task, and develop a plan and project outline. The team will split the work into manageable parts and assign them to group members. Team members get involved not only with their own work, but also with helping others with theirs, so the project can become a true collaboration. One person is often assigned to be the organizer. This person will coordinate the integration of all the pieces into a whole, such as by cutting and pasting the pieces into one write-up, attaching exhibits, and submitting the assignment.

This method has the advantage of getting the entire team involved and receiving contributions from the different experiences and skills of its members. The highest-performing teams tend to be organized this way, probably because of the variety of resources that they are able to tap. This structure also tends to develop a strong group identity, making it easier to work together with each subsequent project. On the negative side, it can be difficult and very time-consuming to turn the work of a number of people into a polished, finished product. In addition, some conflict tends to arise when team members split up the assignment, as some team members will inevitably get assigned the most distasteful portions of the project. For these groups, it is especially important to have an efficient process worked out for splitting assignments equitably and for ensuring that individual team members are living up to their commitments before the submission date.

One project, some team members.
Many groups like to use a hybrid of the first two structures, and assign two or three team members to each project. This is especially popular during time crunches, such as the weeks before finals or during interviewing periods, for groups that prefer to work together but are unable to devote all of their time to every project. Many people feel that this type of team provides a nice balance, providing some of the advantages of each team design. Of course, it also carries some of the disadvantages of each design as well.

On balance, you should experiment with a couple of different team designs early in the semester and try to determine which works best for your team.

CHAPTER 6

Case Analysis

Cases are illustrative narratives of business situations. Usually, you as a student are asked to read ten or twenty pages summarizing the situation, analyze some data, and play the role of a manager by recommending a strategy or plan of action to solve the problem posed. While many other areas of academe rely on textbooks and articles, business education attempts to develop practical skills by including simulations of real-life challenges in the form of cases.

No matter where you go to business school, case analysis will be an important part of your business education, although some schools rely on cases more than others. While textbooks, articles, and analytical tools are excellent ways to learn, business cases provide the unique benefit of putting you in an actual business situation and asking you to think like a manager. Therefore, cases are your chance to apply the academic tools and concepts you have learned in your courses. "In analyzing each case, students learn how to define important issues, when and how to apply analytical techniques, and how to make decisions after evaluating alternatives," notes one U. of Virginia MBA.

Business schools use several different types of cases (most of which are produced at Harvard Business School). Although what follows is by no means an exhaustive list, it will give you a good idea of the types of cases to expect:

The Skill-Builder
Some cases are designed simply to force you to use a particular problem-solving technique. For example, an operations management case may require you to construct a process-flow diagram to find a bottleneck; an accounting case could ask you to calculate cost-of-goods-sold from other data or information; or a finance case could

ask you to calculate the net present value of a proposed investment. These cases are usually shorter and fairly straightforward, since they are really a problem-solving exercise in the form of a business decision.

The Industry Overview

Some cases do not describe a specific situation, but rather describe an entire industry, such as soft-drinks, semiconductors, or toothbrushes. The point here is to encourage you to think strategically and understand a firm from a "macro" perspective, or how the firms in the industry compete with each other. Cases of this nature will usually not ask you to solve a specific problem, but rather act as the basis for exploration of competitive analysis in class discussion.

The State of the Firm

Some cases put you in the shoes of the CEO or high-level executive of a particular firm. This type of case usually traces the firm's history and leaves open a number of challenges for you to think about. Areas of focus may include strategy formulation, international expansion, organizational design and motivation, or the introduction of a new product line. The case may conclude by posing a specific set of questions to be answered, or it may subtly pose issues to be resolved throughout the case. Again, the purpose of this type of case is not so much to solve a specific problem, but rather to get you to think about the series of issues a company must face from a firm-wide perspective.

The Application of a Concept

Despite the more practical nature of today's MBA programs, there are still many theories and frameworks to which you will be exposed, particularly in the area of competitive strategy. Many cases are written to give you a playing field on which to use these tools. For example, a case about Sony may ask you to apply the idea of core competencies; or a case on GE may require the evaluation of different organizational structures.

The Problem and Recommendation

The most exciting cases ask you to explore a pending business decision and make a recommended course of action. By placing you in a mid-level manager's shoes and giving you roughly the same information that you would have in an actual business situation, you learn to think like an executive and get used to the types of problems you will one day face in your job. These cases are usually the most interesting because they force you to analyze a problem in an organized way, apply tools from several classes, and justify your decision to other managers or superiors.

Attacking the Case

Cases vary in their difficulty and time requirements. Some are fairly simple, while others demand a substantial amount of time and energy. The most important thing to remember is that there is no "right" answer to a case. Well-written cases will support several approaches, none of which are necessarily better than the others. The point of the exercise is to get you accustomed to looking at complex problems, considering a number of alternatives, and making a careful decision about which alternative to recommend and why. If you free yourself of the "what's the right answer" approach, you will get more out of the case and be better able to support the course of action you choose. Therefore, don't be concerned if your "solution" to the case differs from the one the professor offers at the end of class discussion.

It helps to have an organized plan of attack in order to make the most of your time. The following is a suggested guide to help you get the most out of your cases in an efficient manner:

1. **Skim the case.** Briefly flip through the reading material, especially the beginning and end portions, to try to get a sense of what are the problems posed and how they might be solved. If there are specific questions posed at the end of the case, briefly read them. This will help you focus on the important parts of the case as you go through it more thoroughly.

2. **Read the case.** The most important objective is to get a general sense of what the case is about so that you can discuss it intelligently. But keep in mind that cases are analytical exercises more than anything else. As you read, highlight what you think are key pieces of information; most cases deliberately have more information than you need for a thorough analysis. Also remember that not everything in a case is an indisputable fact; the casewriter usually wants you to question assumptions and statements, and it's good to disagree

with ideas that others may consider "given." For instance, cases often provide "facts" in the form of opinions offered by some of the company's managers. Feel free to question their opinions. In short, read the case with an independent mind, looking for insights that your unique experience and perspective will make valuable to others.

3. **Identify the issues.** Once you understand the information provided in the case, identify the issues faced by the company or industry. Sometimes there are specific questions posed at the end of the case, or suggested by your professor. Feel free to identify others.

4. **Formulate hypotheses.** Once you have identified the issues posed by the case, you should begin to consider hypotheses for solutions or plans of action. Don't be critical yet. Just think of as many different approaches as possible; the more you have at this point, the more likely you are to understand which one works best for you.

5. **Determine the pros and cons of each.** In your head, on paper, or with your study group, think of the positives and negatives of each alternative course of action. This exercise should start to bring to the surface the key points of analysis in the case. It will also help you decide which course of action you want to recommend.

6. **Decide on a course of action and support your decision with analysis.** When you make your choice of recommendations, remember not to be too concerned about getting the "right" answer. Don't spend too much time deciding which alternative to recommend; how well you support your argument is more important than the argument itself. In fact, an off-the-wall recommendation that is well-supported can score you big points in class discussion. Whenever possible, do some quantitative analysis to back your arguments; most professors love numbers because they are tangible and easy to evaluate, and other students will often neglect to invest their energy in this area.

7. **Get the story straight.** Once you've done all of the above, you should review your work and think about how you will explain your thought process to others in a compelling way. You may have recommendations on a number of issues. Decide on a couple that you feel are the most important.

Class Discussion

Class discussion is the most important part of a case analysis. In the business world, you are going to have to justify many of your decisions orally, and business school is the ideal place to practice. In particular, case discussions force you to be action-oriented in your thought process and to articulate your views persuasively. In addition, as you share views and opinions with your classmates, you will learn from their experiences and develop new approaches to problems. You should use class discussions as an opportunity to fine tune your presentation skills and engage in a productive exchange with other intelligent people.

If you're not prepared for classes, they can be unpleasant experiences. If you don't add anything to the discussion, you may get bored and not get much out of the session. Worse yet, many people live in fear of the infamous "cold call," where the professor calls on an unsuspecting student to present a case or issue to the class. Fortunately, with some preparation before the class, you can organize the issues and your recommendations in advance and be confident in your ability to participate.

The most important thing you can do to prepare is to make sure you have something to say. Review your notes and try to summarize your approach; if you can talk about how you looked at the problem, you should have no problems in class. What is the most interesting thing to you about the case? What do you think is an effective way to approach the problem? What course of action would you recommend first? There are many ways to contribute to the discussion, and these are good starting points.

Most professors are not looking to embarrass anyone, but they do expect you to come to class prepared to talk about the case. You should volunteer to speak up as much as possible, to show that you are learning the material and to decrease the likelihood of being cold-called when you're less prepared. In addition, volunteering also gives you good practice defending your recommendations. Some professors also factor class participation into their grading. Although professors usually rely on volunteers to keep the conversation going, once in a while they will call on students who don't have their hands up, particularly at the beginning of class. Some of their favorite opening questions are:

- What is the state of the industry?
- What are the main issues of the case?
- What alternatives did you consider?
- What do you recommend and why?

If you walk into class with a few key points about the case in mind and a response to questions concerning them, you should be able to relax and enjoy the class discussion.

CHAPTER 7

Key Concepts: Marketing

A business school marketing course deals with how companies design products that satisfy customer demands. Nearly all MBA programs require a marketing course in the first year of business school. Fortunately, most MBAs find it the most interesting required course since it includes sexy topics like advertising strategy and new product launches. This chapter provides an overview of some of the key concepts discussed in an MBA marketing course.

GENERAL MARKETING STRATEGIES

There are several general marketing strategies that different companies tend to use in the marketplace. The four main strategies are as follows:

1. **Low-cost/High-volume.** Companies following this strategy focus on efficient low cost, high-volume production. This strategy tends to be used for commodity products such as rice or paper.

2. **High quality.** Companies that follow this strategy focus on producing the highest quality product possible. Luxury goods manufacturers, such as Rolex or Rolls Royce, often follow this strategy. The danger posed by the "high quality" strategy is that it may lead to "marketing myopia," in which the company focuses so much on increasing the quality of the product that it pays little attention to customers' needs (and whether consumers are willing to pay for such quality).

3. **Aggressive selling.** Rather than making what customers desire, companies following this strategy produce a product or service and then concentrate on actively selling the product to customers. The "aggressive selling" strategy is often used for "unsought goods" like life insurance or water filters. Companies that are faced with excess inventory may also have to adopt this strategy until inventory is reduced.

4. **Find wants and fill them.** This strategy reflects the modern marketing approach and is the strategy your MBA marketing course will likely focus on. This strategy, only recently taught in business school, suggests that rather than concentrating on convincing consumers to want what the company makes, companies should concentrate on making what consumers already want. Therefore, to be successful companies must actively identify the needs of their target market and produce customer satisfaction by tailoring their products and services to fit those needs. Unlike the aggressive selling strategy, this strategy is an "outside-in" approach, since customer demand dictates the type of products or services the firm will provide.

The Modern Marketing Approach

Although the marketing strategy a company may follow for any given product varies, the modern marketing approach taught in business school generally has four major steps: (1) market segmentation; (2) targeting segments; (3) positioning the product or service; and (4) profitability analysis.

1. **Market segmentation.** The first step in a firm's marketing strategy is market segmentation. Market segmentation involves identifying the distinct groups of consumers in the marketplace. There are several ways in which the company can divide (or "segment") the market, including geographically, by income, age, gender, buying habits, or by "user status" (such as frequent users, moderate users, and non-users). Segments should

be easily measurable, homogenous within each segment, and distinctive relative to other segments.

Once the company has identified these distinct groups (or "segments"), the company can determine the different needs or wants of each of the groups. One way to do so is to construct a "typical" member of the segment and then ask what this person would want.

Example: A hypothetical clothing company named Calvin Stine Fashions is considering launching a line of denim jeans. Based on its research, Calvin Stine decides that the best way to segment the jeans market is by age: 12-29, 30-50, and 50 and older. Since these segments tend to have different tastes in jeans, buying habits, and price sensitivity, the company's approach is probably an effective way to segment the jeans market. The company then conducts research to determine what the typical member of each segment looks for when he or she buys jeans.

---

2. **Targeting segments.** Once the company has identified the segments in the market and the characteristics of each segment, the company must now decide which of these segments it will target. Successful companies realize that they cannot realistically serve every market segment, so they are better off selecting a few segments and serving them well. The first step in choosing which market segments to target is measuring each segment's *attractiveness*. Factors to consider in determining a segment's attractiveness include: whether the segment already contains aggressive competition; the threat of new entrants into the segment; and whether buyers are price sensitive or have strong bargaining power. Having identified the most attractive segments, the company must then determine whether it has the business capabilities needed to serve these segments. Finally, the company selects among the attractive segments based on business capabilities.

Example: Assume that Volkswagen Motors performs a market segmentation of the American car market. The company identifies three major segments: economy car buyers, middle market buyers, and high-income car buyers. After analyzing the segments' attractiveness, the company determines that economy car buyers and high-income car buyers are the most attractive segments (e.g., because economy car buyers are the largest segment and have the potential for higher volume, and because high-income car buyers generate higher profit margins). However, after looking honestly at its business capabilities, Volkswagen may decide to target the economy car market because it may lack the business capabilities to serve the high-income market.

3. **Positioning the product.** Once the company has selected which segment (or segments) to target, it must then design the product to meet the needs of its target segments. Designing the product to fit the needs of the company's target segments is called *product positioning.* Product positioning involves differentiating the company's products from those of its competitors by tailoring its marketing-mix (also known as "The Four P's": product, price, place, and promotion) in response to the segment's attributes.

Example: Assume that the Calvin Stine clothing company (above) decides to target the 12-29 year old segment of the jeans market. Calvin Stine must then tailor its marketing-mix (i.e., product, price, place, and promotion) to appeal to its target segment. First, the product itself must be designed with the target segment in mind (for example, more slim design, stone-washed, etc.). Next, the jeans must be priced with the segment in mind (for example, priced higher than the competition to convey an image of quality and prestige). In addition, the places, or channels, where the jeans are to be sold must be selected to appeal to the segment (for example, prestigious department and specialty stores, but avoiding discount stores, to maintain an image of exclusivity). Finally, the promotional campaign will be designed to appeal to the segment, so avant garde ads in fashion *magazines may be most effective. In sum, the jeans will be specifically designed and positioned to appeal to the company's target segment.*

4. **Profitability (the Fifth P).** Finally, the company must determine the profitability of any marketing undertaking. Before a company launches a new product or promotional campaign, it must ask itself whether it will likely make money as a result. One way to determine profitability is to conduct a *break-even analysis*, which asks: how many more unit sales must the marketing effort generate in order to pay for itself? This Break Even Volume is calculated by dividing the marginal profit on each unit sold (or "contribution margin") by the fixed costs of the marketing effort. Once the Break Even Volume is determined, the company must decide how likely such sales volume would be. If the probability is low, the company may have to abandon its proposed marketing plan.

Example: *Calvin Stine determines that its new product launch would cost $25,000,000. It has also determined that the sales price of its jeans would be $40, and that each pair of jeans will cost $15 to make, so the contribution margin per jean is $25. The Break Even Volume is therefore $25,000,000/ 25 = 1,000,000 jeans.*

Faced with this number, however, the company realizes that one million jeans would be a 25 percent share of the designer jeans market, which the company feels is unrealistic. Therefore, the company may decide to abandon its new product launch.

Satisfying Customers

Much of the focus in a first year MBA marketing course will be on how firms create customer satisfaction. Business schools now teach that consistently delivering customer satisfaction is the most important determinant of a company's long-term profitability.

Whether a customer is satisfied after purchasing a product depends primarily on the product's performance relative to the buyer's expectations. Expectations that are too high may result in dissatisfied customers. The most successful companies create high expectations in their customers and then meet these expectations.

It is also important that companies carefully track their customers' level of satisfaction by using, among other tools, customer hotlines and customer surveys, and by conducting an analysis of why "lost customers" stopped using the company's products or services. Companies must constantly determine to what extent their customers are satisfied or dissatisfied with the company and why so that they can fix what is wrong and continue what is working.

Retaining Customers

Your business school marketing course will also likely address strategies for customer retention. Successful businesses realize that it always costs more to attract a new customer than it does to retain a current customer. A satisfied, repeat customer generates increased profits for the firm because he provides word-of-mouth advertising for the company, his purchasing transactions become standardized and less costly (e.g., he already has a customer account on file, etc.), and he is more loyal to the company and therefore less price sensitive.

The main steps for identifying and improving a company's retention rate include: (1) measuring the company's retention rate, (2) identifying the major causes for customer defections, (3) determining how much profit the company loses when it loses a customer (i.e., determining the customer's "lifetime value"), and (4) calculating how much it would cost to reduce the defection rate and whether this cost is less than the customer's lifetime value.

Once the company has identified its retention rate and the causes for customer defections, the company can implement several strategies for improving customer retention. First, it may create financial benefits to the customer that encourage retention (such as frequent-flier programs or cash-back bonuses). The company may also personalize the service so the customer feels special (for example, a "preferred customer card" with certain perks). The company may also establish switching barriers to retain customers (such as a long-distance company's imposing a fee to switch to another provider). However, the most effective and lasting way to improve customer retention is to satisfy customers consistently.

CHAPTER 8

Key Concepts: Statistics

BASIC STATISTICS CONCEPTS

If you're entering business school without a quantitative background, you may find the notion of statistics difficult at first. However, statistical analysis will soon pervade nearly all of your other B-school courses and most case analysis. Here's an overview of some of the basic statistics concepts you'll be expected to know.

Displaying Data

One of a manager's primary functions relating to statistical data is preparing the data for display to others (such as a supervisor or a client). For example, a product manager who has conducted some market research will seek to present the data in a manner that is easy for her supervisor to understand. Two popular methods for displaying data in a visual way are *histograms* and *scatter plots*.

An example of a histogram might be as follows. This histogram displays the percentage of entering MBA students who are in various age groups:

Figure 8-1: Histogram

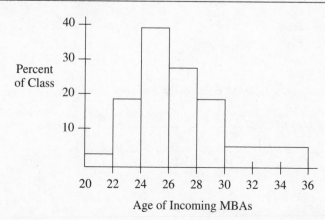

Age of Incoming MBAs

An example of a scatter plot relating MBA students' prior years of work experience to their starting salary upon graduation might be as follows:

Figure 8-2: Scatter Plot

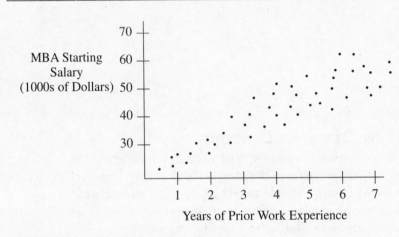

Mean

Once you have displayed the data, your next goal as a manager will be to interpret it in a meaningful way. Managers interpret data using various summary statistics, the most basic of which is the *mean.*

The mean (or average) of a set of numbers represents the "center" value of the set. The mean is calculated by summing up the numbers and dividing by how many numbers there are.

Example: Assume that the first year class of a (very) small business school has the following GMAT scores:

540

570

580

600

630

690

The mean GMAT score of the first year class is:

$$PV = \frac{540 + 570 + 580 + 600 + 630 + 690}{6} = \frac{\$3,610}{6} \approx 602$$

Standard Deviation

Another important summary statistic managers use is the *standard deviation*. The standard deviation of a set of data measures the data's spread around the mean, or how far away from the average the data tend to be. Although there is a formula for calculating standard deviation, in business school you will usually use statistical software programs, such as Execustat or DataDesk, to calculate the standard deviation of a set of numbers.

Normal Distribution

If the data regarding a population is gathered randomly, a plot of the data should approximate a *normal distribution* (or "bell-shaped" curve), which is about equally distributed on either side of the mean. The curve of the GMAT scores of a business school's first year class might look like this:

Figure 8-3: Normal Distribution

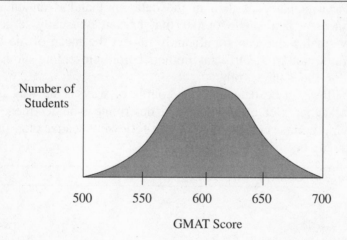

The mean GMAT score of this class is about 600, with students' scores about equally distributed on both sides of the mean.

Standard Deviation and a Normal Distribution

If the data approximates a normal distribution, we will expect about *two-thirds* of the data to fall within one standard deviation from the mean. In addition, we will expect about 95 percent of the data to fall within two standard deviations from the mean, and 99 percent of the data to fall within three standard deviations from the mean.

Example: *If a business school's MBA class has a mean GMAT score of 600, with a standard deviation of 30, we would expect that:*

- *About 67 percent of the students have a GMAT score between 570 and 630 (plus or minus one standard deviation from the mean).*
- *About 95 percent of the students have a GMAT score between 540 and 660 (plus or minus two standard deviations from the mean); and*
- *About 99 percent of the students have a GMAT score between 510 and 690 (plus or minus three standard deviations from the mean).*

Outliers

An *outlier* is a piece of data in the data set that has an unusual value. Since even a single outlier that has an unusually large or unusually small value can significantly impact the mean of the data set, it is important to identify any outliers before presenting summary statistics of the data to others.

An outlier can be detected in a couple of ways. One way is to look at a scatter plot of the data and determine whether there are any outlying points. For example, in the following scatter plot, point A appears to be an outlier:

Figure 8-4: Outlier

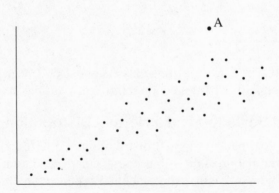

To determine whether an extreme point is indeed an outlier, you can ask whether the point is more than three standard deviations from the mean. (Remember that we expect over 99 percent of all points to be within three standard deviations of the mean.)

If you locate an outlier, you should be suspicious. For instance, an outlier that is more than three standard deviations away from the mean is not likely the result of random variation. Therefore, there is probably an explanation for the unusual value, like a transcription error. If the outlier proves to have been an error, it should be removed from the data set.

Correlation

Correlation measures the strength of the relationship between two variables. The strength of the correlation is measured by the *correlation coefficient* (r), which has a value between −1.0 and 1.0. A correlation coefficient of 1.0 indicates a perfect positive correlation between two variables (for instance, the correlation between the age of a child and his height). A correlation coefficient of zero indicates that two variables have no correlation (for instance, the correlation between a child's blood type and his height). A correlation coefficient of −1.0 indicates that two variables have a perfect negative correlation (for instance, the correlation between the age of a child and the number of cartoons he watches on television). Values in between −1.0 and 1.0 indicate various levels of strength of a correlation, or lack of it.

Regression Analysis

The foundation of any business school statistics course is *regression modeling*. Regression modeling involves the use of a mathematical equation to represent the relationship between two variables ("X" and "Y"). The regression equation can then be used to predict Y by plugging in various values of X. Therefore, businesses can use regression models to predict figures into the future, such as sales or product demand, using various X variables (such as weather, unemployment rate, etc.).

We arrive at the regression line by "fitting" the best line to the data as seen in Figure 8-5.

Figure 8-5: Regression Line

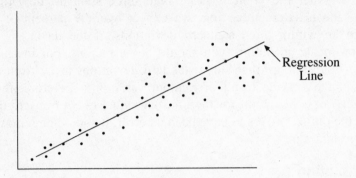

The regression line is simply the line that best fits the data. The equation of the regression equations takes the form of:

Y = a + bX

where: Y = the y-axis variable (the variable we want to predict)

X = the x-axis variable (the variable we will use to predict Y)

b = slope of the regression line

a = the y-intercept

Example: Chicago Motors, an automobile manufacturer, wants to better predict its monthly automobile sales so that it can plan production accordingly. After conducting research, Chicago Motors determines that the primary determinant of the company's auto sales are market interest rates. The company gathers sales data for the past year and plots the monthly car sales of its dealers against market interest rates:

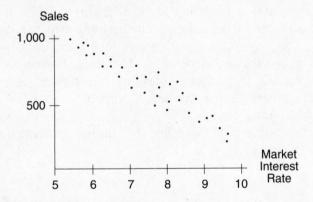

The company then fits a regression line to the plotted data as follows:

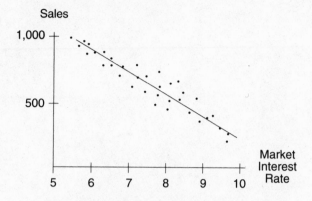

The equation of the regression line is: Sales = 1000 − 50i (where i = the interest rate). If market interest rates are currently at 9 percent, Chicago Motors can predict that this month's sales will be:

$$Sales = 1,000 - 50(9) = 1,000 - 450 = 550 \text{ cars}$$

R-squared and Outliers

A statistic called the *r-squared* measures how well the regression line predicts the value of Y. An r-squared close to 100 percent indicates that the model has very high predictive value. Conversely, an r-squared close to 0 percent indicates that the model is virtually useless.

In regression modeling, it is especially important to detect and eliminate outliers. Even one or two outliers can seriously affect the equation of the regression line by pulling the line up or down toward the outlying point. Often you will find that eliminating an outlier will substantially improve the model's r-squared value.

CHAPTER 9

Key Concepts: Operations and Manufacturing

UNDERSTANDING OPERATIONS

Most MBA students have no intention of managing a production line for a living when they graduate. However, the operations function of a company is often the crucial determinant of its profitability, and more and more high-level executives are paying attention to operations as an important driver of corporate success. The trend is to look at production not merely as a cost center, but rather to view it as the integration of all functions that provide service to the customer. It is crucial for any graduate business student to have a good understanding of operations to be able to see the whole picture of an integrated company.

An operations management curriculum is often divided into three primary areas of focus. *Process analysis* examines the manufacturing process and tries to improve production speed and efficiency. *Supply and demand coordination* determines the best level of output given uncertain demand. And *process control* measures the quality of output and tries to isolate the sources of and reasons for defects in production.

Process Analysis

A process is anything that takes inputs (raw materials, brainpower, etc.) and combines or reorganizes them in a way that produces something of greater value. A process can be a manufacturing process, such as the production of automobiles, or it can be a service process, like the delivery of overnight mail. Businesses have developed a widely recognized approach to describing and analyzing processes that allows them to monitor and improve productivity.

In order to visualize the way a process works, managers will develop process flow diagrams. Process flow diagrams visually break down each step of a process and order them from start to finish:

Figure 9-1: Process Flow Diagram

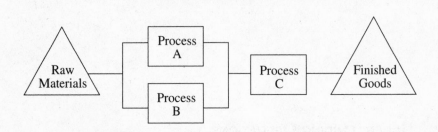

Note that rectangles represent tasks and triangles represent inventory, or storage of goods. Storage of information, such as orders or routing procedures, is represented by a circle.

In addition to using diagrams, operations managers use a number of terms to describe the nuts and bolts of a process:

- *Setup time* is the time needed to get a process ready for production. For example, a factory usually has to set the dyes in its machines before it can begin to run materials through them.

- *Throughput time* is the time it takes for a unit of production to go from the beginning of the process to the end of the process. If twelve ounces of cola takes five minutes to go from a vat of liquid into a finished, sealed can, the throughput time for the canning process is five minutes.

- *Cycle time* is the amount of time that passes in between units that come through the process. Even though it takes five minutes for a can to go through the canning process, you can send more than one can through the process at a time. If a can comes off the line every two minutes, then the cycle time for that process is two minutes. Note that there is not necessarily a relationship between throughput time and cycle time.

- A *bottleneck* is a limiting step in a process. Usually, the slowest step (or the step with the longest cycle time) is a bottleneck because it limits how fast inputs can go through the process. After the first unit goes through, the cycle time of the bottleneck will be the cycle time of the process as a whole.

- The *capacity* of a process is the number of outputs the process can produce in a given period of time. *Utilization* is the percentage of capacity that is being produced within that time.

When analyzing a process in business school, you must break it down into its separate steps and calculate cycle times for each. Then you can calculate capacity and investigate ways to improve output or utilization. For example, say you discover the following cycle times in the above-mentioned canning process:

Step A (machine): cycle time = 8 minutes

Step B (labor): cycle time = 3 minutes

The bottleneck is step A, because it takes longer than step B, so the cycle time of the entire process is eight minutes. While the labor in step B can handle one can every three minutes, it must wait for step A to finish. After the first unit's throughput time, a finished unit will come out of this process every eight minutes. Assuming the process runs for eight hours (480 minutes) per day with no setup time, then the capacity is sixty units per day.

What if you want to improve the capacity of the process? Adding another laborer to step B wouldn't help, because step A would still be the bottleneck. But if you add another machine to step A, the cycle time is reduced to four minutes. Although step A is still the bottleneck, cutting its cycle time in half doubles daily capacity to 120 units.

If you add another machine to step A the cycle time for A becomes two minutes. Note this reduction changes the bottleneck of the process from step A to step B, and the capacity becomes 160 units (eight hours divided by three minutes per can).

Supply and Demand Coordination

Companies must continuously make decisions about how much of their products they want to produce. This task is particularly challenging for products that take a long time to produce and have uncertain demand, like personal computers, cars, and books. Managers must balance the risk of missing sales opportunities by not producing enough of the product with the risk of booking inventory losses by producing more than they can sell.

While there is no way to predict demand perfectly, there are a number of methods designed to help managers make intelligent decisions based on known information. The most frequently cited method is called the "Newsboy Model," so named after a story of a boy who sells newspapers and who must change the way he orders from his publisher.

After years of being able to return unsold newspapers for a full refund, a change in corporate policy at the newspaper publisher forces the boy to pay in advance for all the newspapers he orders without the opportunity for a refund. Because demand for newspapers fluctuates a great deal from day to day for reasons such as changes in weather and the interest-level for headline stories, it now becomes crucial for him to develop a method for determining the right number of newspapers to order each day.

Clearly, there is much more at stake in his forecasting exercise now than there was when he could get a refund. Now if he orders too many papers, the boy will lose money on the ones he doesn't sell. If he doesn't order enough, he will lose profitable sales and, potentially, long-term customers who get angry when he is out of stock.

In order to determine a good order level for such a situation, you must try to weigh the potential lost profit with the potential gained profit. To do so, you need three pieces of information: (1) the profit you make from selling a paper, (2) the loss you take from failing to sell a paper you have ordered, and (3) the probability of selling various amounts of papers.

Once you know this information, the optimal order amount can be determined using formulas from microeconomics. Remember that the ideal output point is where marginal revenue equals marginal cost, or the point where the expected profit is highest. If you are one newspaper below this point, you are leaving profits on the table; if you are one above this point, you are eating into your sales.

The optimal number of newspapers to order can be determined with an expected profit analysis. Assume that a paper costs you $0.25 to buy, and that you can sell it for $0.50. You therefore know that each paper you sell gives you a profit of $0.25, and each one you fail to sell loses you $0.25. Assume also that after tracking your sales for the last few months, you have estimated the following probabilities of selling a certain number of papers on any given day:

Sales	Probability
0	0%
100	20%
200	35%
300	20%
400	15%
500	10%

The way to approach the problem is to determine the greatest number of papers you can order where the expected profit from selling the last paper you buy is greater than the expected loss from not selling all the papers you buy.

In this example, you know you should order at least 100 papers, because you have a 100 percent chance of selling at least 100. What happens if you add 100 papers to your order, making it 200? You have an 80 percent chance of selling the extra hundred, making your expected profit 80% * (100 * $0.25) = $20.00. You have a 20 percent chance of not selling it, making your expected loss 20% * (100 * $0.25) = $5.00. Because your expected gain is greater than your expected loss, you should order at least 200 papers.

But if you go up to 300 papers, the picture changes. Your gain from the extra hundred is 45% * (100 * $0.25) = $11.25, while your loss is 55% * (100 * $0.25) = $13.75. Here, your loss is greater than your gain, so you shouldn't increase your order to 300. The optimal order, then, is 200 newspapers.

It turns out that there is a handy formula for determining the correct order level. You should order the greatest number of the product such that:

$$p \geq \frac{c_o}{(c_o + c_u)}$$

where p is the probability of selling at least a given number of units;

c_o is the cost of ordering one too many; and c_u is the cost of ordering one too few.

Of course, the probabilities of the different sales levels as outlined in the chart above are not always readily or accurately available. Companies today use a variety of methods to estimate demand, including historical sales, customer surveys, trial introductions, and others. While their methods are not perfect, they can usually make good working estimates to factor into their optimal purchasing and production plans.

Quality Control

Another aspect of operations management is quality control. Quality is not an absolute concept; no company can make perfect products 100 percent of the time. Nor do many companies strive for 100 percent perfection, since achieving a higher perfection rate costs money. Quality is instead a relative measure, one that measures output against the needs of the target market. For someone buying a luxury car, the "quality" of her purchase is much more important to her than it is to someone buying a utility vehicle. But the utility purchaser may be happier with her purchase than the luxury person, because her *relative* expectations are met or even exceeded. In this case, the utility vehicle may be of higher quality than the luxury vehicle.

One measure of quality is called a defect rate, which measures the percentage of defective products that come off the line. While companies can strive for a 0 percent defect rate, there is a cost trade-off between lower defects and cost. The fewer defects you want, the more you have to spend on quality control (like product inspections).

Another technique is called statistical process control, or SPC. SPC starts with the premise that no two outputs coming out of a process will be exactly the same; there is always some randomness in production. A company sets its machines or processes to achieve certain specifications or target levels, and it must decide on an acceptable level of variation for its machines; the less variation, the more expensive the machine. For example, a high-quality stereo manufacturer must meet very high specification levels with great consistency; its customers will expect high-performance products. But a more mainstream producer will set lower levels, perhaps with less consistency, because for its customers price is more important than technical superiority.

The issue, then, is how to measure the consistency with which a product meets its design specifications, and how to tell if a process is "in control" and producing merely random variations, or is systematically not staying within acceptable ranges of variation. SPC first uses probability theory to determine the range of variation in a process that can be attributed to randomness as opposed to a true flaw. Specifically, the concept of a normal distribution curve is used to calculate upper and lower control limits for the amount of variation that is considered a "normal" part of the process.

As discussed in chapter 8, a normal distribution curve is a theoretical curve that represents the distribution of random events. The idea is that in a random process, the most frequent outcome will be the mean, or average, and the rest of the outcomes will occur with symmetrical variation on either side of the mean. A normal distribution curve looks like this:

Figure 9-2: Normal Distribution

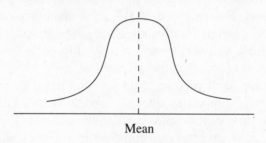

Mean

The standard deviation, or sigma, is a measure that helps determine the scale of the horizontal axis, or the size of the acceptable variations from the mean.

A company can then use the normal distribution curve to calculate numerical limits on how much variation its processes should have. If, upon sampling a number of units off the production line, variation stays within these limits, then the process is "in control," producing a statistically acceptable number of differing products. If, however, the variation goes outside the limits, or shows some kind of trend, then a problem likely exists and needs to be investigated. Companies will actually sample output and plot measurements on a control chart like this:

Figure 9-3: Control Chart

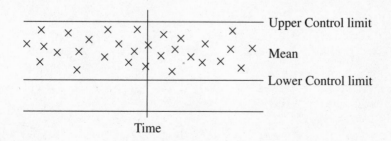

Time

In this case, the variation appears to be within acceptable limits.

The challenge for many operations managers is to narrow the space between control limits and achieve consistent levels of quality. One such method, developed recently by Japanese companies, is called Just-in-Time inventory, or JIT. JIT operates under the premise that inventory is bad because it uses up capital and costs money. Moreover, inventory can hide defects in a process because you might not notice them if you throw them into a big storage room with a bunch of unused parts or outputs.

JIT tries to eliminate inventory as much as possible by coordinating all the steps in the supply chain so that everything appears as needed and when needed. For example, a JIT auto manufacturer will sign agreements with a small number of parts suppliers to continuously ship parts in small numbers every day. As the parts come in, they are immediately sent through the production line, where they move through every step with precise timing. When the cars are finished, they are promptly shipped to dealers, who have placed orders for specific models in quantities to meet their customers' demand.

Of course, zero inventory is impossible in practice, but many manufacturing companies have implemented it as a goal because of its many benefits. It allows for better monitoring of quality, because defective parts are noticed immediately. It saves money, because not as many parts have to be stored. And it allows for greater flexibility in the manufacturing process, because orders can be changed easily to respond to changes in demand or seasonality.

Just-in-Time does have its drawbacks, of course. It places a lot of pressure on a small number of outside suppliers, and if they can't meet their promises, the whole production line can stall. It is also very stressful for workers, who are allowed virtually no slack time. It is a risky strategy, but it is one that has enormous financial benefits if implemented well.

CHAPTER 10

Key Concepts:
Competitive Strategy

FORMING A COMPETITIVE STRATEGY

Many people believe that competitive strategy is the most interesting area of business because it requires the incorporation of all the different functions of a company into a coherent, understandable vision. The strategist is ultimately responsible for the direction of the firm, and must think like a CEO in formulating strategic objectives and developing a plan for implementing them. In business school, you will use concepts drawn from all of your other courses in trying to evaluate and design strategies for a number of different companies, ranging from Fortune 500 conglomerates to entrepreneurial start-ups.

Competitive strategy is a broad discipline and is not easy to define. Most business-school classes, however, will focus on a few introductory topics: industry analysis, core competencies, organizational design, and strategic alliances.

Industry Analysis

When looking at a particular industry as either an established competitor or as a potential entrant, a manager must ask the question: "Is this a good business for me to be in?" While there are an infinite number of ways to answer this question, a number of tools have been developed to help the practitioner approach the issues in an organized way. The most frequently used method, the "five-forces" analysis, was introduced by Michael Porter, a Harvard Business School professor, in his landmark book *Competitive Strategy*.[1]

Porter presented five key determinants of competitive interaction, applicable to any industry, and organized them into an easy-to-use framework for assessing the position of the competing firm. These five forces are:

1. The threat of new entrants into the industry

2. The threat of substitute products

3. The bargaining power of suppliers

4. The bargaining power of customers

5. The rivalry among industry players.

By thinking about the nature of an industry in terms of the relative attractiveness of these five factors, one can make an assessment about how successful a company could be given the type of market it is trying to enter.

For example, based on this model, the personal-computer hardware industry looks like a particularly uninviting industry for a new entrant. It requires moderate amounts of capital for a new entrant to get into the business, thus making even a successful firm vulnerable to new competition at almost any time. New, more advanced hardware comes to market very frequently, while the value of established brand names is eroding, establishing a serious threat of a substitute product. While suppliers of hardware manufacturing know-how may be plentiful, the consumer usually has a wide choice of products from which to choose, making price cuts likely. Finally, the players in the industry now are extremely competitive, and have been known on occasion to resort to ruthless tactics to sell their products. Not an appealing place for an established firm, let alone an unassuming start-up!

The soft-drink industry, by contrast, looks pretty good for the established players. The high-capital costs necessary for economies of scale, combined with the enormous value of existing brand names, make it difficult for new entrants to compete effectively. While common sense may dictate that other liquid nourishment (like spring water or fruit juice) could substitute for soft drinks, the longevity of consumer preferences for particular drinks argues to the contrary. Suppliers like sugar growers have little power because most of the ingredients are widely available commodities. And buyers are dispersed all over the world and would have difficulty organizing into any powerful negotiating body. If the competitors can refrain from killing each other with price wars, it looks like a very good business to maintain a strong position.

The five-forces model has become the cornerstone of any strategic analysis, and is used by students and practitioners alike. It is an extremely valuable tool, one that you will use far beyond your business school education.

Core Competencies

In their acclaimed article "The Core Competence of the Firm,"[2] Gary Hamel and C. K. Prahalad introduced an influential language to begin talking about firm capabilities. Companies should define themselves, the authors argued, not merely on the basis of the products they currently sell, but on the resources and capabilities that give them a sustainable competitive advantage. This will help them anticipate changes and trends in the marketplace and be flexible enough to take advantage of situations where they have the wherewithal to be profitable. It further allows them to formulate a strategy that maximizes the use of their unique set of resources.

For example, the horse-buggy companies of the nineteenth century viewed themselves as companies that sell horse-buggies. While not an untrue statement, it proved to be quite damaging from a competitive standpoint. Really, what they sold was ground transportation. When the automobile was introduced in the twentieth century, a superior alternative for ground transportation became available and horse buggies became obsolete. By defining their core competence too narrowly, they failed to keep themselves open to substitute products. They were of course put out of business because their product was no longer useful.

This concept of the core competence of a firm has led companies to redefine themselves on a regular basis, and in some cases shed business operations that are not part of their "core" business. It has also become particularly popular in formulating strategy for mergers and acquisitions. The conventional wisdom nowadays is that for an acquisition to be successful, the acquiring company must bring some resource to the target firm that will make it more valuable than it would have been in someone else's hands. The classic, modern example of this phenomenon is Disney's purchase of Capital Cities/ABC. Disney's core competence was in developing entertainment programming, but it was not strong in distribution; Capital Cities was exactly the opposite. By combining the two, they could complement each other's strengths and potentially create a whole that is more valuable than the sum of its parts.

Organizational Design

Another important aspect of company success is the fit between organizational structure and strategic goals. There are many ways to organize a firm: centralized, decentralized, divisionally, geographically, flat, hierarchical, and so on. None of these is clearly superior to the others, but each of them will be right for some companies but dead wrong for others.

Take, for example, a start-up technology firm. Because of the importance of creativity and product development, a flat structure with very little hierarchy and an open exchange of ideas from all employees could be a very successful mode of organization. Because the company is probably growing very rapidly, with the prospect of high earnings for all employees, people are very willing to play multiple roles and work as one team to achieve a common goal. Also, because most employees probably know each other, it is easy to form a cohesive unit where people can see and understand what is going on in all areas of the company.

As the firm grows, however, and stops expanding at such a rapid rate, it becomes more difficult to maintain such an environment. For one thing, the new size makes it difficult to monitor the entire firm, and without a system of controls, the organization could turn chaotic. Also, as more people join the firm, the atmosphere becomes less congenial, as people lose touch with some parts of the company. For a bigger company, control is perhaps the most important issue to consider when implementing an organizational structure.

Global companies have another set of issues to worry about. Because of the nature of national and geographic differences among cultures, some products may not be as popular in one country as they are in another; at the very least, particular features may be more important to one group than to another. This would suggest that a company should manufacture products specifically for each country in which it sells. On the other hand, one of the benefits of a big, global organization is the economies of scale that come with increasing volume. By dispersing manufacturing facilities, the company may lose this competitive advantage. Therefore, there is a necessary trade-off between local market expertise and volume-production savings, and a company must balance the benefits of each.

In short, different organizational designs can work well in different situations. A company must look at its line of business, its size, its people, and its growth rate to determine the most appropriate fit for its particular strategic plan.

Strategic Alliances

As business becomes more complex, and as companies become more specialized in their services and products, it is increasingly difficult for start-up operations to enter new businesses or areas. Knowledge about local markets and flexibility to meet a wide variety of client needs become crucial determinants in defining competitive success.

When a firm wants to enter a new market, one of the options it should consider is forming a strategic alliance with another company that may have the expertise that it lacks. In so doing, the firm can complement its skills without a major investment, and increase the likelihood of success because of the strengths and resources of its partner. Strategic alliances are becoming more and more popular in a broad range of industries.

For example, if a company wants to introduce a product in a country where it has never done business before, it can enter into a partnership with a local firm that has, say, distribution networks and a sales force already set up for the product that the foreign company wants to sell. By combining forces, the company can bring a new product to market faster and more effectively than either one could do on its own. The cost, of course, is that it will have to share some of the profits of the venture. But often this cost is offset by the reduced risk that comes with investing less money over a shorter period of time.

Alliances are also popular when companies want to bring new products in their home countries into markets or industries that they have never been in before. For example, a chemical company may ally itself with a pharmaceutical distributor to help market a drug that it inadvertently discovered in some of its research.. Rather than set up an infrastructure for a pharmaceuticals division, it can piggyback on the already established distribution network of its partner.

The success of many alliances remains a hotly debated question. Do they really make companies more profitable? On one hand, they make firms more flexible, because by matching up complementary strengths, firms can make the best use of their unique sets of resources. In truth, however, alliances are very difficult to maintain successfully. This is largely because of the difficulties inherent in working with other parties who have different long-term goals. While it is necessary to share knowledge and information to further the cause of the alliance, it can be harmful to share too much information with a potential competitor. A company does not want to let all of its know-how and technological expertise flow to another company because of loose controls in an alliance. Many alliances break up because of disagreements between the partners.

Alliances are good ways to enter new lines of business while minimizing the capital outlay and, hence, the risk of the venture. However, the parties must negotiate a very clear agreement that spells out unambiguously the rights and obligations of each partner.

END NOTES

1. The Free Press, New York, 1980.

2. *Harvard Business Review*, May-June 1990

CHAPTER 11

Key Concepts: Finance

FINANCIAL DECISION MAKING

Your first-year finance course deals with the decisions that financial managers of companies must make. For example, a financial manager must decide whether to make a particular expenditure, such as an investment in a new project, piece of equipment, or new factory. Financial managers must also decide whether to raise new capital by issuing debt or stock, and whether the firm should pay dividends to the shareholders.

Present Value

The concept of present value is based on the notion that a dollar received one year from now is worth less than a dollar received today. As a result, a sum of cash to be received in the future must be discounted in order to arrive at its value in today's dollars (i.e., its present value).

Figure 11-1: Present Value of a Future Cash Flow

$$PV = \frac{C^t}{(1 + r_t)^t}$$

Where: C^t = A cash flow received t years from now

r = Discount rate

Example: *Assume that your uncle offers to pay you $1,000 three years from now. Also assume that the discount rate (r) is 6 percent. The present value of the future cash flow is:*

$$PV = \frac{\$1,000}{(1.06)^3} = \frac{\$1,000}{(1.06)^3} = \$840$$

For now, don't worry about how to arrive at the proper discount rate (r) to use when figuring the present value. This is discussed later in the chapter.

Present value of a series of cash flows

In business, you will often be asked to calculate the present value of a series of future cash flows. To determine the present value of a series of cash flows, you simply discount each cash flow separately and add up the present values:

Figure 11-2: Present Value of a Series of Cash Flows

$$PV = \frac{C_1}{(1+r)} + \frac{C_2}{(1+r)^2} + \frac{C_3}{(1+r)^3} \cdots \frac{C_t}{(1+r)^t}$$

Where: C^t = The cash flow in year t

r = Discount rate

Example: Muffy has a trust fund that will pay her $1,000 one year from now, $1,500 two years from now, and $2,000 in three years. Assume that the discount rate (r) is 6 percent. The present value of Muffy's trust fund payments is:

$$PV = \frac{\$1,000}{1.06} + \frac{\$1,500}{(1.06)^2} + \frac{\$2,000}{(1.06)^3}$$

$$= \$943 + \$1,335 + \$1,679$$

$$= \$3,957$$

Perpetuity

A cash flow received each year forever is called a perpetuity. To solve for the present value of a perpetuity, you would technically have to discount each year's cash flow and add up the present values! Fortunately, there's a short cut. The present value of a perpetuity can be seen in Figure 11-3.

Figure 11-3: Present Value of a Perpetuity

$$PV = \frac{C}{r}$$

Where: C = The cash flow each year
r = Discount rate

Example: John is considering taking a year off of work to write a novel. Based on his agent's projections, John expects to earn $1,000 in book royalties every year forever, starting next year. Assume that the discount rate (r) is 6 percent. The present value to John of writing the book is:

$$PV = \frac{\$1,000}{.06} = \$16,667$$

Growing perpetuity

In business, most perpetuities are in fact growing perpetuities. That is, the sum of cash to be received each year increases by a particular percentage (known as "g" or "the growth rate"). The present value of a growing perpetuity is:

Figure 11-4: Present Value of a Growing Perpetuity

$$PV = \frac{C}{(r-g)}$$

Where: C = The cash flow in year 1
r = Discount rate
g = Growth rate

Example: Assume that John, the novelist, expects to earn $1,000 next year. However, after the first year, the book's price (and therefore John's yearly royalty) is expected to increase by 4 percent per year. Assume that the discount rate (r) is 6 percent. The present value of the book to John is:

$$PV = \frac{\$1,000}{(.06-.04)} = \frac{\$1,000}{.02} = \$50,000$$

Net Present Value (NPV)

Perhaps the most important type of decision financial managers must make on a daily basis is whether to undertake a proposed investment. For example, should the company buy a certain piece of equipment? Build a particular factory? Invest in a new project? These types of decisions are called capital budgeting decisions. The financial manager makes such decisions by calculating the net present value of each proposed investment and making only those investments that have positive net present values.

The net present value (or NPV) of an investment is simply the present value of the series of cash flows generated by the investment, minus the initial investment:

Figure 11-5: Net Present Value

$$NPV = -C_0 + \frac{C_1}{(1+r)} + \frac{C_2}{(1+r)^2} + \frac{C_3}{(1+r)^3} \cdots \frac{C_t}{(1+r)^t}$$

Where: C_0 = Initial investment

C_t = Cash flow in year t

r = Discount rate

Example: *Steinberg is the CFO of Eastern Motors Corp., an automobile manufacturer. The company is considering opening a new factory in Michigan, which will require an initial investment of $1 million. The company forecasts that the factory will generate after-tax cash flows of $100,000 in Year 1, $200,000 in Year 2, $400,000 in Year 3, and $400,000 in Year 4. At the end of Year 4, the company would then sell the factory for $200,000. The company uses a discount rate of 12 percent. Steinberg must determine whether the company should go ahead and build the factory. To make this decision, Steinberg must calculate the net present value of the investment. The cash flows associated with the factory are as follows:*

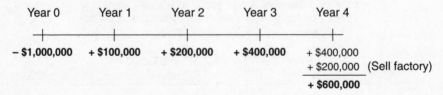

Steinberg then calculates the NPV of the factory as follows:

$$NPV = -\$1,000,000 + \frac{100,000}{1.12} + \frac{200,000}{(1.12)^2} + \frac{400,000}{(1.12)^3} + \frac{600,000}{(1.12)^4}$$

$$= -\$1,000,000 + \$89,286 + \$159,439 + \$284,712 + \$381,311$$

$$= -\$85,252$$

Since the factory has a negative net present value, Steinberg correctly decides that the factory should not be built.

The net present value rule

Note from the example above that once the financial manager has figured out the NPV of a proposed investment, she then decides whether to undertake the investment by applying the net present value rule:

Make only those investments that have a positive net present value.

As long as the financial manager follows this rule, she can be confident that each investment she undertakes is making a positive net contribution to the company.

The Capital Asset Pricing Model (CAPM)

So far, we have been assuming a given discount rate in our examples. However, part of a financial manager's job is to determine an appropriate discount rate (r) to use when calculating net present values. The discount rate may vary depending on the investment.

Beta

The first step in arriving at an appropriate discount rate for a given investment is determining the investment's riskiness. The market risk of an investment is measured by its beta. A well-diversified portfolio of stocks, such as the Standard & Poors 500, has a beta of 1. Therefore, an investment with a beta of 1 has the same riskiness as the market as a whole (so, for example, when the market moves down 10 percent, the value of the investment will on average fall 10 percent as well). An investment with a beta of 2 will be twice as risky as the market (so when the market falls 10 percent, the value of the investment will on average fall 20 percent).

CAPM

Once the financial manager has determined the beta of a proposed investment, she can then use the Capital Asset Pricing Model (CAPM) to calculate the appropriate discount rate (r):

Figure 11-6: Capital Asset Pricing Model

$$r = r_f + B(r_m - r_f)$$

Where: r = Discount rate

r_f = The risk-free rate of return

r_m = Market rate of return

B = Beta of the investment

The risk-free rate of return is the return the company could receive by making a risk-free investment (for example, by investing in U.S. Treasury bills). The market rate of return is the return the company could receive by investing in a well-diversified portfolio of stocks (for example, the S&P 500).

Example: Anderson, Inc., a coal producer, is considering investing in a new venture that would manufacture and market carbon filters. Anderson's chief financial officer, Fuqua, wants to calculate the NPV of the proposed venture in order to determine whether the company should make the investment. After studying the riskiness of the proposed venture, Fuqua determines that the beta of the investment is 1.5. A U.S. Treasury note of comparable maturity currently yields 7 percent, while the return on the S&P 500 stock index is 12 percent. Therefore, the discount rate Fuqua will use when calculating the NPV of the investment will be:

r = .07 + 1.5 (.12 − .07)

= .07 + .075

= .145

= 14.5%

Although this is an overly simplified discussion of how financial managers calculate discount rates to use in their cash-flow analyses, it does give you an overview of how managers incorporate the notion of an investment's market risk to select the appropriate discount rate.

Future Value

We can also take a sum of money today and calculate how much it will be worth in the future.

Figure 11-7: Future Value

$$FV = C(1 + r)^t$$

Where: C = The value of the cash flow now

r = Interest rate

t = The number of years into the future

Example: *Josephine Wharton deposits $1,000 into a bank CD which pays 6 percent per year for the next five years. The value of Josephine's investment after five years will be:*

$$FV = \$1,000(1 + .06)^5 = \$1,338$$

Compounding

So far we have assumed that the discount rate or interest rate was compounding annually. In many cases, however, the rate is compounded semi-annually (twice a year), quarterly (four times a year), or monthly. In these cases, you must convert the annual rate into an equivalent rate compounded monthly, quarterly, etc. The future-value conversion equation can be seen in Figure 11-8.

Figure 11-8: Future Value compounded p times per year

$$FV = C \left(1 + \frac{r}{p} \right)^{pt}$$

Where: C = The value of the cash today

r = Annual interest rate

p = Number of interest payments per year

t = Years into the future

Example: *Josephine Wharton deposits $1,000 into a bank CD which pays 6 percent per year, compounded semi-annually, for the next five years. The value of Josephine's investment after five years is:*

$$FV = 1,000 \left(1 + \frac{.06}{2} \right)^{2 \times 5}$$

$$= 1,000 \, (1.03)^{10} = \$1,344$$

Notice that this value is slightly higher than the value of the investment when compounded annually.

Valuing Bonds

The value of a bond is the present value of the cash flows associated with the bond, discounted at the market rate of return (r). This is the same as finding the present value of a series of cash flows, except that the cash flows are now simply the bond's interest payments and the return of the principal when the bond matures.

Example: *Sloan is considering purchasing a $10,000 bond that has a 7 percent coupon, which is paid at the end of every year. The bond matures in exactly five years, and market interest rates are currently 8 percent. Sloan must determine the price she is willing to pay for the bond.*

The cash flows associated with the bond are as follows:

Year 1   Year 2   Year 3   Year 4   Year 5

| — | — | — | — | — |

+ \$700   + \$700   + \$700   + \$700   + \$700
                                                    + \$10,000 (Bond matures)

                                                    + \$10,700

Sloan may now calculate the present value of the bond's cash flows, discounted at the market interest rate, as follows:

$$PV = \frac{\$700}{(1.08)} + \frac{\$700}{(1.08)^2} + \frac{\$700}{(1.08)^3} + \frac{\$700}{(1.08)^4} + \frac{\$10,700}{(1.08)^5}$$

$$= \$648 + \$600 + \$556 + \$515 + \$7,282$$

$$= \$9,601$$

Therefore, Sloan should be willing to pay \$9,601 for the bond.

Valuing Stocks

The value of a stock equals the present value of the stock's future dividends. Therefore, assuming the stock will pay dividends in perpetuity, the present value of the stock is:

Figure 11-9: Present Value of a Stock

$$PV = \frac{DIV}{r}$$

Where: DIV = Next year's dividend
r = Discount rate

More commonly, a stock's dividends can be projected to grow at some constant rate (g). Therefore, the value of a stock can be determined using the following formula for a growing perpetuity.

Figure 11-10: Value of a Stock with Growing Dividends

$$PV = \frac{DIV}{r - g}$$

Where: DIV = Next year's dividend

r = Discount rate

g = Dividend growth rate

Example: XYZ Corp. stock will pay a dividend next year of $2 per share. XYZ is a mature company and its dividend is expected to grow by 5 percent per year. Assume that the appropriate discount rate is 12 percent. The present value of a share of XYZ stock is:

$$PV = \frac{\$2}{.12 - .05} = \$28.57 / share$$

Modigliani-Miller (MM)

Another important decision financial managers must make is whether to raise new capital by issuing debt or stock. Two theories you will surely learn in your finance course are the well-known Modigliani-Miller (MM) propositions regarding the capital structure of companies.

MM Proposition I states that the value of a firm is unaffected by its capital structure (i.e., its mix between debt and equity). Therefore, MM I says that a company cannot increase its value simply by choosing to issue more debt instead of more equity (or vice versa).

MM Proposition II states essentially the same principle by observing that as a company's debt level increases, investors require a higher rate of return. As a result, the value of the company remains constant.

It is important to note that these MM propositions depend on several assumptions that do not necessarily hold true in the real world. For example, issuing debt generates tax shields that may increase the value of the firm, while issuing stock does not.

CHAPTER 12

Key Concepts: Economics

MICROECONOMICS

For all you quant-o-phobes out there, microeconomics is just about your worst nightmare. It is by far the most math-intensive subject in any MBA core curriculum—including finance—and it requires a lot of problem-solving work just to keep up with the main concepts. It is a demanding subject, but it is very helpful in understanding how businesses make decisions.

Microeconomics is the study of how people and firms behave economically. It tries to explain the forces that shape markets from both a consumer and a company standpoint: how pricing and production decisions are made, how supply and demand equilibrium is achieved, how decisions of one firm affect those of other firms, and so on. While a thorough treatment of the subject would require a chapter the length of a Ph.D. dissertation, the following overview should give you a good introduction to the main concepts of the subject as taught in business school.

Supply and Demand

The basic idea of supply and demand says that prices affect the quantities of goods bought and produced. In general, the lower the price of a particular good, the more consumers want to buy; the higher the price, the more producers want to sell. The price at which the quantity supplied equals the quantity demanded represents the market equilibrium, and is usually where the prices and outputs will stabilize. Supply and demand are represented on the following graph of the price of a good versus the quantity supplied or demanded.

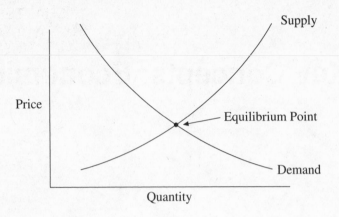

Note that movements along the supply or demand curves do not represent changes in supply or demand; they are merely changes in price or quantity. If supply or demand changes (say, because the product suddenly goes "in" or "out" of style), the whole curve moves, and the equilibrium point changes to a new price and output level. For example, if the above demand curves shifts to the right, this means that at every price, consumers demand more of the good. In this case, both price and quantity will rise because the new intersection is up and to the right of the old one.

Price Elasticity

Price elasticity is a measure of how significantly changes in price affect supply and demand. Companies pay particular attention to price elasticity of demand because it helps them determine the most profitable price to place on their product. Understanding how changes in price affect demand is crucial to achieving maximum profit levels.

Some products are very sensitive to changes in price. Take a luxury good such as premium wine. Many people do not buy premium wine because it is expensive. They would like to buy it, but they don't want to spend a lot of money on it because they can buy other types of wine for a lot less. But if the price were to drop suddenly, more people would buy it because the price would be more affordable to them. Conversely, the more expensive it is, the fewer the number of people that will choose to buy it since people can easily live without premium wine. Therefore, premium wine is an example of a good with highly elastic demand.

Other products are not very sensitive to price changes. For example, the demand for emergency heart surgery is not likely to change very much no matter what the price. People who need heart surgery are willing to pay almost anything to have it. They will not demand more of it if the price drops, and they will not demand less if the price increases. Similarly, college textbooks are not very sensitive to price changes. If the price of a required textbook is raised one year from $40 to $60, nearly the same number of students will buy the book. Similarly, if the price were to fall to $20, approximately the same number of books would still be sold. Therefore, heart surgery and textbooks are examples of products with highly inelastic demand.

An important point to remember is that elasticity is not the same at all prices of a good. If premium wine, for example, costs $1 per bottle, a 50 percent change in price is not likely to have much of an effect on the quantity of wine demanded. But if it costs $50 per bottle, a 50 percent change will probably have a much bigger effect on quantity. Therefore, any measure of price elasticity is usually considered to cover only small changes in price.

Production and Competitive Markets

Presumably, companies try to make as large a profit as possible. In order to do so, they must make decisions about how much of their products to produce and the prices at which to sell them. While a popular strategy might be to produce and sell as much of the product as possible, this is not always the most profitable strategy. Companies must understand how their production and pricing decisions affect their bottom line. Because of the relationship between supply, demand, price, and output, they use microeconomics to do so.

A company's cost of producing a good depends in part on how much of that good it produces. If only a small number of goods are produced, then it usually costs more, on average, to produce each good. This happens because the fixed costs that are incurred regardless of production levels are spread out among very few goods. In contrast, the more goods that are produced, the lower the average cost. But if a company tries to produce too much of the good, the average cost will probably go up again, because employees and machines will be running into each other on the production floor.

A graph of average cost versus quantity is therefore U-shaped, like this:

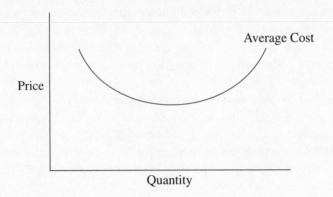

Companies, however, do not make pricing decisions based on average cost. They make production decisions based on a concept called marginal cost. Marginal means "for one more." The marginal cost of production is the cost of producing one more of a good. For example, if a company makes 100 radios, the marginal cost would be the cost of producing the 101st radio. Like the graph of average cost, the graph of marginal cost is U-shaped, but it looks a little different:

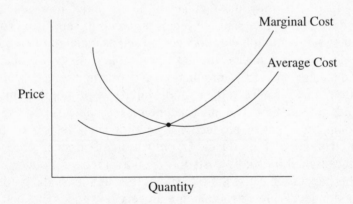

The marginal cost curve always crosses the average cost curve at the bottom of the average cost curve. This is because when the cost to produce one more good is less than the average cost, the average cost will decrease; when it is greater, the average cost will increase.

The concept of marginal cost is important because a company wants to produce at an output level so that every last good it produces is profitable. This means that the price the company receives for a good should be greater than the cost to produce it. In a perfectly competitive market, all companies must sell their goods at the market price; the price is therefore given as a horizontal line. The point where price equals marginal cost represents the greatest possible output level where production is still profitable.

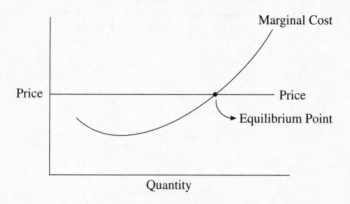

Because most of the marginal cost curve is upward-sloping—costs are going up as you increase production—the intersection of price and marginal cost is a dividing point, and represents the profit-maximizing output. To the left of the point, with lower production, price exceeds marginal cost, making each additional good profitable. To the right, with higher production, marginal cost exceeds price, making each additional good unprofitable. Therefore, in a perfectly competitive market, a company will produce at the output level where the last good produced is the last possible profitable good—where price equals marginal cost.

However, most markets are not perfectly competitive. They are monopolistically competitive. This means that differences exist among similar goods produced by different companies, and although people can buy goods produced by other companies, they can't buy the exact same good. Take a Mercedes-Benz, for example. People can buy many types of cars. But they can't buy a Mercedes from anyone but Mercedes-Benz. In such markets, the price of a company's product is not a given; it depends in large part on how much they produce. This makes predicting revenues a little more difficult.

Companies in monopolistically competitive industries therefore need to consider marginal revenue in their pricing and output decisions.

Marginal revenue is the additional revenue the company gets from selling one more good. Marginal revenue usually decreases as quantity increases because in order to sell more, the company has to lower its prices. Therefore, marginal revenue is not equal to price, because in order to sell one more good the company has to lower the price on all goods. This means that your price, or average revenue, goes down with each additional good you sell. The marginal revenue curve will therefore look like this:

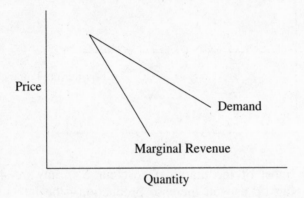

Note that the marginal revenue curve has twice the slope of the demand curve.

In monopolistic competition, companies will produce at an output level where the marginal revenue equals the marginal cost. To the left of this intersection, the additional revenue from one more good is greater than the cost, making it worthwhile to continue production. To the right, cost is greater than revenue, making additional output undesirable.

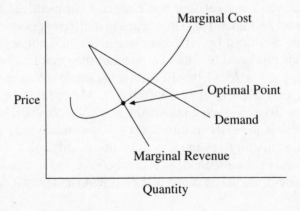

Game Theory

Game theory is one of the most interesting topics in microeconomics. Game theory will not teach you how to win at blackjack or craps, as the name suggests, but it will help you think about corporate decisions in the context of a competitive, dynamic environment.

Game theory starts with the assumption that everyone in a competitive situation is about as smart as you are. That is, other firms are trying to maximize profits, and they have roughly the same brainpower and resources that you do. The odds are good that you're not going to outsmart anybody just by doing what's in your own interest. A well-managed firm, therefore, takes into account the actions and reactions of its competitors before making its major decisions.

For example, say you are a producer of paper towels in competition with one other firm. Right now, your prices and your competitor's prices are exactly the same. You feel that you could afford to lower prices a little bit, given your cost structure and profit requirements. You decide that if you lower prices, you will gain customers and profits, because consumers will want to buy your paper towels for less than they can buy your competitor's. So you lower your prices five cents a roll.

If you use this reasoning, what you fail to take into account is the potential reactions of your competitor. It is true that they might feel that they can't lower prices any further, and keep them at the higher price. But the chances are good that once you lower yours, they will lower theirs as well. There is even a possibility that they will lower them even more than you do, starting a price war that could do serious damage to both firms.

Game theory tries to put these competitive situations into a mathematical framework with something called a payoff matrix. A payoff matrix depicts the decisions competitive firms can make and the corresponding payoffs, taking into account the decisions the other firms can make. Take, for example, the paper towel example above:

Competitor

		Keep	Cut
You	Keep	15, 15	–25, 25
	Cut	25, –25	–10, –10

The matrix is read from left to right. That is, the number on the left in each box is the payoff to you, and the number on the right is the payoff to your competitor.

Note that in this example, no matter what your opponent does, you are always better off cutting prices. If your opponent keeps his prices the same, you will make 25 if you cut your prices; you will make only 15 if you don't. If your opponent cuts prices, you will lose 10 if you cut prices as well; you will lose 25 if you don't. This means that cutting prices is your dominant strategy, and you will choose it every time. Assuming your opponent will choose it too (he has the same payoffs that you do), you both lose 10 instead of potentially gaining 15 each.

This type of situation, where both players choose a harmful strategy because each doesn't trust the other, is called a prisoner's dilemma. Advanced game theory considers such issues as how firms can signal to each other that they are going to follow the "good" strategy. This can be a daunting task, because price-fixing and signaling can violate anti-trust laws.

CHAPTER 13

Key Concepts: Accounting

There are two major categories of accounting taught in business school: financial accounting and cost accounting. Financial accounting provides information about the company to external users, such as investors, lenders, and regulatory agencies. Cost accounting provides information about the company for internal users for managerial decision making.

FINANCIAL ACCOUNTING

Financial accounting is prepared for external users using Generally Accepted Accounting Principles (GAAP). By requiring that all firms use the same accounting rules, GAAP is designed to create some uniformity among the financial statements of different companies. However, GAAP still provides firms with lots of leeway in preparing their financial statements.

The three principal financial statements discussed in business school are the Balance Sheet, the Income Statement, and the Statement of Cash Flows.

Balance Sheet

A firm's balance sheet lists the company's assets and sources of financing (such as debt and equity) as of a particular date.

Figure 13-1: Balance Sheet

Anderson Software, Inc.
Balance Sheet
December 31, 1995
(in thousands of dollars)

Assets		Liabilities	
Cash	$10,000	Accounts Payable	$25,000
Accounts Receivable	25,000	Notes Payable	10,000
Marketable Securities	5,000	Long Term Debt	5,000
Property, Plant, and Equipment	5,000	Total Liabilities	$40,000
Total Assets	**$45,000**	**Shareholders' Equity**	
		Common Stock	$5,000
		Total Liabilities and Shareholders' Equity	**$45,000**

Accounting Identity

Notice that in the above balance sheet, the sum of the firm's assets exactly equal the sum of its liabilities and equity. This is the accounting identity, and it always holds true for any firm:

$$A = L + E$$

where: A = assets

L = liabilities

E = equity

Another way of stating this principle is to say that the firm's assets must equal the claims on those assets (by creditors and owners).

Income Statement

The second major financial statement is the income statement. A firm's income statement lists the firm's revenues, expenses, and net income over a period of time (such as a quarter or a year). A sample income statement may look like this:

Figure 13-2: Income Statement

Anderson Software, Inc.
Income Statement
For the Year Ended December 31, 1995
(in thousands of dollars)

Sales	$50,000	
less: Cost of Goods Sold	(15,000)	35,000
less: Selling, General and Administrative expenses		(15,000)
Net Income Before Taxes		20,000
less: Income Taxes		(8,000)
Net Income		**$12,000**

Statement of Cash Flows

The third major financial statement is the statement of cash flows. A firm's statement of cash flows lists the firm's sources and uses of cash over a period of time (such as a quarter or a year). The firm's cash inflows and outflows will be grouped into three major categories: cash from operating activities, cash from investing activities, and cash from financing activities.

Figure 13-3: Cash Flow Statement

Anderson Software, Inc.
Cash Flow Statement
For the Year Ended December 31, 1995
(in thousands of dollars)

Cash from Operating Activities:

Net Income	$12,000
Increase in Accounts Payable	4,000
Increase in Accounts Receivable	3,000
Increase in Inventories	(3,000)
	+16,000

Cash from Investing Activities:

Sale of Building	$4,000
	+4,000

Cash from Financing Activities:

Repayment of Long Term Debt	(3,000)
Sale of Building	1,000
	(2,000)
Cash Flow	**$18,000**

COST ACCOUNTING

Cost accounting is the use of financial and accounting information for managerial decision making. It differs from financial accounting in that financial accounting focuses on presenting information to people outside a company, while cost accounting uses accounting information presented to those inside a company, such as managers, to help them make operational decisions. For example, a plant manager must decide which mix of products has the most efficient cost structure. A sales manager must decide which customer accounts are the most profitable given the company's constrained capacity. A good manager must know how to estimate and measure financial performance in order to understand the factors that influence these decisions.

Believe it or not, cost accounting is not the most boring subject in business school. In fact, many MBA students think it is one of the most fascinating and useful subjects they learn about in B-school.

Almost every business person will use cost accounting at some point in his life. It is a consummately practical subject that focuses on real-life problem solving. And contrary to popular belief, it is not a particularly math-intensive subject. What quantitative work there is can be handled easily by an average high-school student. It is more conceptual than it is mathematical.

An introductory cost-accounting class will cover four main topics: (1) general cost allocation, (2) activity-based costing, (3) variance analysis, and (4) executive compensation. Cost allocation is the process of determining how much a particular product or service costs to provide. Activity-based costing is a new development that attempts to measure cost information by measuring the cost of the different activities in the production process. Variance analysis compares actual performance to budgeted performance and tries to isolate the sources of the difference. Executive compensation designs links between pay and corporate performance in a way that is beneficial to owners, shareholders, and executives.

Cost Allocation

Every company wants to know how profitable its products are. If a product sells well and costs little to make, the company should make more of that product. If another product sells well but costs a lot to make, the company may consider selling less of it. Unfortunately, when a single company makes a variety of different products, it often has trouble determining exactly how much each of its products really costs to produce and, as a result, how profitable each of its products really is.

For example, a company may manufacture nails and screws in the same factory. Some costs, like the raw materials used to make the products, are easily calculated: you know how much metal is in each nail or screw, and you know how much that metal costs to purchase. But other costs are more difficult to determine because it is not clear how much cost is "used up" by each particular product. For example, money paid for factory rent is a cost that should be borne by both nails and screws. Clearly, both products use the factory. But how much of it do they use? How much rent is used to make screws, and how much to make nails? More specifically, how much rent is used for each nail and each screw? In order to get a complete picture of the cost structure, a manager must provide answers to these questions.

Cost allocation is the art of determining how these costs should be divided up among the different products. "Allocation" means calculating expenses and assigning them to products based on the amount of those expenses that they use. It is an art because there is no way to know the precise answer, so the best you can do is estimate. Each person in an organization will have her own ideas regarding how costs should be divided up among different products.

The most important thing to know about cost allocation is knowing the difference between the various types of costs: variable costs, fixed costs, direct costs, and overhead costs.

Variable costs increase with the number of products produced. These costs are usually easier to handle because they often can be directly attributable to a particular product. Fixed costs, however, are incurred regardless of the number of products produced. Fixed costs are usually the most difficult to allocate because it is not clear to which products they should be allocated and how much.

Direct costs are manufacturing costs that can be directly attributed to a particular product, such as labor hours spent operating a machine that makes nails. Overhead costs are costs that are necessary to the production of the product, such as plant maintenance or corporate managerial staff, but are not directly attributable to the objects themselves. Overhead costs can be either fixed or variable. For example, corporate accounting staff is variable; the more products you make, the more you need to account for them. The plant manager's salary, however, is largely fixed; no matter how much you produce, you still have to pay the manager. Overhead costs are usually the most difficult to allocate.

These different types of costs are incorporated into two methods of calculating net income. The gross margin, or full absorption, approach is similar to the way net income is calculated in financial accounting:

Revenue

Less Cost of Goods Sold (COGS) = Gross Margin

Less Nonmanufacturing Expenses = Net Income before Taxes

Note that in this method, COGS includes both fixed and variable costs; it is everything incurred in manufacturing, including factory overhead. Nonmanufacturing includes corporate expenses, and these also may be fixed or variable. The gross margin approach is not very popular in cost accounting because it makes it difficult to allocate expenses to particular products.

The other approach is the contribution margin, or direct, method, which separates costs into variable and fixed costs:

Revenue

Less Variable COGS

Less Variable Nonmanufacturing = Contribution Margin

Less Fixed COGS

Less Fixed Nonmanufacturing = Net Income before Taxes

This method is more popular in cost accounting because it offers more valuable managerial information. When a manager has to make production decisions, she usually looks at variable costs more than fixed costs. This is because there is nothing you can do about fixed expenses in the short run; you are going to spend them regardless of how much you produce. Variable costs, on the other hand, help you determine how much profit you will make at different production levels.

When determining the profitability of particular products, you must allocate overhead costs to each one. This is not an easy task, and there are many ways to do it. Corporate overhead can be allocated by number of products produced, number of products sold, direct materials cost per product, revenues per product, and so on. A bad decision about how to allocate these costs can make products appear more or less profitable than they really are. For instance, if a company makes both gold bars and iron bars and allocates its costs based on revenues per bar, it is likely to get a misleading indication of the true cost to produce a bar. Even though the gold bars do cost more, the extra cost comes mostly from the higher price of raw materials; there is probably very little difference in the true cost of production once you adjust for this difference.

The manager, then, must decide which allocation method makes the most sense for each overhead cost. Common sense and thorough knowledge of the production process is usually enough to help make that decision. A company may have many different overhead pools, and it can allocate each one however it thinks it should. Remember that no method for cost allocation is infallible. When allocating costs, the manager tries to make the production process much simpler than it probably really is. But in the end, a well-thought-out allocation system can give a pretty good indication of the profitability of a company's products.

Activity-Based Costing

One method for cost allocation that has become particularly popular over the last decade is activity-based costing, or ABC. ABC is simply one approach to cost allocation, but it is viewed separately from other cost-allocation systems because it has been used frequently in conjunction with business re-engineering, a very popular concept in corporate America.

ABC breaks business processes into activities and assigns costs based on these activities. Instead of allocating production costs based on volume or dollars or anything else, ABC allocates costs based on the different activities necessary to produce a product. The ABC accountant must trace every activity in the production process, from materials procurement through manufacturing, sales, and customer service. He then must decide how much each of these activities costs. Once these values are determined, the production process for each product can be outlined by the number of activities involved, and the cost for each product can be ascertained with a good degree of accuracy.

ABC accounting is particularly useful for companies that make a wide variety of products because it attempts to measure the corporate resources that each product uses on a real-time basis. It also helps managers determine which steps of their production processes are particularly costly. By breaking down the operation into activities, and measuring how much these activities cost, ABC helps highlight processes that may be particularly expensive or inefficient. Managers can then "re-engineer" their production process to cut out unnecessary waste.

Variance Analysis

Every company makes a budget to help plan its operating activities and production needs. Budgets are commonly set at the beginning of the calendar or fiscal year and updated monthly. The budgeting process usually involves people from corporate planning, operations, and finance.

Once a budget it completed, it is used not only for planning, but also for performance measurement. If a company does not meet its profit targets, it needs to know whether the shortfall resulted from too few sales or from too many expenses. Likewise, if it exceeds its profit targets, it wants to make sure it understands why so that it can continue to improve.

The difference between actual performance and budgeted performance is called a variance. For example, if it costs $20,000 to make your products in a given month but you had projected $25,000, you have a negative variance of $5,000. Revenue variances are broken down into price variance and volume variance. Some of the variance may result from unexpected changes in price (price variance); the rest results from differences in sales volume (volume variance).

Cost variances are much more difficult to calculate, mostly because there are so many reasons why costs can fail to meet projections. To help break these reasons down into more manageable pieces, cost accounting compares actual results to two different budgets. The first, the master budget, is the original cost estimate for the budgeted production volume. The second, the flexible budget, is the cost estimate revised after-the-fact to reflect the actual production volume.

For example, if you budgeted that it would cost $10 to make a radio and you expected to make 100 radios, you would have a budget of $1,000 for radios. This is your master budget. If you really made only ninety radios, then your flexible budget is $900. The difference of $100 is called the sales volume variance. This variance is important because it separates differences in costs into differences that result from volume and differences that result from operational, or process-oriented, factors, which are more controllable from the production manager's standpoint.

Once you know your flexible budget, you can compare it to your actual performance to determine the causes of your variance. In the example above, say you made ninety radios and your actual costs were $1,100. Although your master-budget variance is $100 ($1,100 minus $1,000), your flexible-budget variance is $200 ($1,100 minus $900). This means that after adjusting for differences in volume, your operating costs were $200 higher than they should have been.

The flexible-budget variance is further broken down into a price variance—the variance resulting from differences in prices of inputs—and an efficiency variance—the variance resulting from differences in the amount of each input required to complete the job. By breaking variances down into these different categories, a manager can isolate reasons for increased costs and locate areas for improvement.

Executive Compensation

Another use for all of this cost information is the measurement of profits for determining executive compensation. If you're as ambitious as most MBA students are, you may want to know how you're going to be compensated someday when you're a CEO, or at least a high-level manager. Although business school will not negotiate your salary in advance for you, it will help you understand what goes into compensation packages so that you can design the best plan for your company and for yourself.

Most senior executives are compensated at least in part based on the financial performance of their companies. The question is, how should financial performance be measured? Many CEOs have pay packages that are linked to the market price of the company's stock. For them, this is probably a good system. But for middle managers, you need to find a measurement that is more closely linked to events that are within their control. The theory is that if a manager is rewarded based on the quality of his performance, he will have more incentive to do his job well and help the company as a whole.

The problem is, of course, that the theory is difficult to execute in practice because true employee performance is difficult to measure. Accounting measures like net income, average cost, or total revenues are common measuring sticks. But a manager's division can do well or poorly because of factors that are beyond her control. Should a regional vice president be rewarded just because her area had unprecedented population growth? Furthermore, if managers are measured by yearly data, as accounting data usually is, doesn't this provide an incentive for them to plan for the short run instead of for the long run? Finally, setting up performance-measurement systems based on financial data provides opportunities for managers to "game the system" and figure out ways to make it look like they are doing better than they really are. These issues need to be considered before implementing a particular incentive plan.

By the same token, accounting measures are often reliable measures of executive performance. Surely there is some relationship between accounting profit and managerial ability, even if it isn't a one-to-one relationship. And accounting profit is relatively easy to compute; it doesn't cost a fortune to develop complicated measurement systems that may not be right anyway. All in all, executive compensation plans related to performance measurement must be watched and tweaked with a careful eye, but they have been embraced in some form by almost all of corporate America.

CHAPTER 14

Recruiting

When applying to business school, you probably made it sound like you have known exactly what you wanted to do with your career ever since you were ten years old. Now that you're in, however, you are free to admit the truth: that while you probably have a pretty good idea of what your long-term goals are, you can't decide exactly what field you want to get into right out of business school. In fact, you might not even have a clue.

Fortunately, you've come to the right place, because recruiting at most business schools is designed for people who have only loosely defined career objectives. Contrary to popular belief, business school is not populated with sons and daughters of CEOs who have been trained ever since they were two years old to go work for McKinsey. Most students in fact do have ambitious goals, but they are largely unformed. They have come to business school to learn about the opportunities that are out there and to expand their universe of options.

Over the course of your MBA education, you will probably learn as much about the careers that are available to you as you will about management. You will be bombarded with information about companies, careers, job search strategies, and, we hope, job offers. At the end of the road, you will have learned more than you can imagine about yourself and what you want out of your professional life.

While this book is not meant to be a career guide—your career office will have a wide range of resources available for you—it can provide you with an insider's perspective of what to expect during the MBA job search. What follows is a guide to help you understand how the process works so that when the time comes, you can be prepared to get as much as you can out of it.

STEP ONE: PRESENTATIONS AND RECEPTIONS

Starting relatively early in the school year and continuing throughout the recruiting season, most of the companies that hire MBAs will come to campus to make a pitch. Sometimes the pitch will be in the form of informational flyers in your student mailbox or mailfolder. Other times, the pitch will be in the form of a booth at a business school career fair. The company may also come to campus and put on a "corporate presentation," in which company executives deliver polished talks, sometimes complete with a slide show, asserting that their firm offers the best opportunity, challenge, and rewards that you will be able to find anywhere. Afterwards, they may host informal receptions, complete with cocktails and hors d'oeuvres, where students can meet employees of the firm (usually recent graduates of the school), who will invariably talk about how fantastic it is to work at the firm.

You should, of course, take these events with a grain of salt, since they are meant to "sell" you on the company. However, they are also great opportunities to learn more not only about a particular firm, but about an entire industry. If you're not sure what commercial banking is all about, for example, go to a few presentations, and after a while you should get a good sense for the different job functions. Many times the presentations reveal a lot about the culture of the company and the types of people it attracts. The receptions allow you to have some real-life interaction with company representatives and will give you a pretty good feel for the type of work they do and the types of people they hire.

There are two schools of thought on the importance of these presentations. One view is that the presentations don't matter a bit in the recruiting process, since the companies generally use the time to speak in favorable generalities and don't really want to talk to you up close until interview season begins. The other is that they are crucial elements in the recruiting game, and opportunities for job offers can be won or lost based on the contacts you make at the receptions.

Reality lies somewhere in the middle, but overall corporate presentations are opportunities you should definitely take advantage of. While you need not attend a firm's presentation to land a job offer from the company, it can normally be a big help. Often, the company employees present at the reception are the ones sent to campus to interview prospective applicants, and it lays a foundation for a good interview to have met the interviewer informally at the firm's reception. It is true that some firms, particularly the most prestigious ones, probably couldn't care less whether you go to their reception; they know that most people are interested in working for them, and they probably won't learn much about your talent standing over a vegetable plate. But most take your presence as a sincere sign of interest and, come interview time, will refer to the reception's sign-in list for an indication of who has been faithful.

The receptions are also a great chance to make a friend at a company you are particularly interested in. While conversations in these settings are usually not enough to land you a job, it can't hurt to have at least one person who might remember your name and face—especially when resumes are being reviewed to compile interview lists or extend offers for call-back interviews. Sometimes a short note or a follow-up phone call to a person with whom you had a good rapport can go a long way toward getting you in the door.

While it is good to be outgoing, however, do not try too hard to impress at a company event. Receptions are meant to be informal and nonevaluative, and someone who comes on strong can appear obsequious and do more harm than good. The individuals who work for these companies are just like you; they like people who are intelligent and have enthusiasm, but they don't like brown-nosers. In short, relax, enjoy yourself, meet some people, but don't knock yourself out.

STEP TWO: NETWORKING AND INFORMATIONAL INTERVIEWING

Corporate presentations are only one way to gather information about the careers and companies that interest you. Once you have a good idea of the types of jobs you would like to pursue, it is a good idea to start talking to people who are currently in those fields. In this way, you can find out more about what the jobs are really like and whether they are right for you. Also, you can establish early relationships that may eventually pay off in a job opportunity.

This process is usually referred to as "networking," but really it is just a way for you to talk to some people who know a lot about what you are trying to do. Many times, recent alumni are more than willing to talk to you for a few minutes and give you some advice; your school's career center should have directories available for you. "Access to alumni is very easy and very helpful," confirmed one NYU MBA. Personal contacts, friends, and former business associates can also be great sources of information. "You're constantly networking and meeting potential employers," reported one Columbia MBA. You should ask as many questions as you can think of, not only to get information, but also to show that you are serious and interested.

Another technique is called "informational interviewing." Many students like to set up face-to-face meetings with employers where they can get to know people in a more personal way. While they are meant to be nonevaluative, information-gathering sessions, be aware that people will always draw conclusions about you. Prepare as you would for a "real" interview.

Again, while many people downplay the importance of networking, it is clearly one way of differentiating yourself and getting the inside track on interviews and job opportunities. Once you get out of business school, it will be your primary source of job leads for the rest of your career. In sum, you should definitely talk to as many people in the "real world" as you can. Not only will they give you the inside story, but they may actually help you get a job when the time comes to hand out offers.

STEP THREE: RESUMES AND COVER LETTERS

Odds are, by this time you know how to make a resume, and you've written plenty of cover letters in your day. Presumably, you had to do both to get your first job. But at business school, the stakes are higher, and the players are a lot more sophisticated. You need to have a perfectly polished paper presentation to be effective in the MBA job market.

Again, this book is not meant to be a how-to career guide. Every business-school recruiting office has its own particular format for how to write a resume, and you should follow the style that they recommend. But there are a few general rules that you should remember as you put your professional life story onto a single piece of paper:

- **An MBA's resume should under no circumstances be longer than one side of a page.** When a recruiter looks at a resume, she wants to see important information quickly. If she has to wade through a bunch of peripheral detail in order to get to what she's after, she's not going to be interested for too long. If you keep your resume to one page, you will do a good job of emphasizing the important details of your experience without boring the reader with extraneous detail.

- **Portray yourself in the most positive light—don't be afraid to brag!** If you don't show off your good points, no one else will, so make sure to put all of your best features on your resume. Don't assume that you'll be able to tell your "real" story in the interview, because you might not even get that far. If you got 800 on the GMAT, put it down. If you were the number one analyst in your class, say so. If you fly German warplanes in your spare time, make sure anyone reading your resume knows it. This is not the time to be modest. All information is relevant if it helps convey an understanding of your talents and personality.

- **Whatever you do, always tell the truth.** Although this should go without saying, we all are tempted to make our last job sound just a hair more substantial than it was. While there is nothing wrong with emphasizing your strengths and playing down your weaknesses, make sure that you can substantiate everything on your resume with facts. People do check into your background, and the last thing you want is to lose a job opportunity because the five people who you said reported to you really reported to your boss.

As far as cover letters go, your career office will again have recommendations about the format you should use. Here are a few tips on your cover letter you should keep in mind regardless:

- **A cover letter should look like business correspondence.** While this sounds obvious, you need to make sure that your cover letters look like polished business letters. This means printed on a laser printer, with no spelling errors and good grammar. Don't take the little things for granted, because you may be judged in part on the basis of your written communication.

- **Make sure you are sending the letter to the right person.** A simple phone call to make sure that the recruiting coordinator you met is still in that position can go a long way toward avoiding a minor embarrassment. Remember that people change jobs often, and the person whom you should have sent the letter to six months ago might not be the same person you should send it to now. Check the spelling of the person's name while you're at it.

- **Highlight something unique on your resume.** The goal of the cover letter is to get the reader interested in you. To this end, you should pick out something in your background that is relevant to the job you are applying for and say a few words about it in the letter. You don't have to tell your life story, but you should convey something that distinguishes you from the hoard of letters that every hiring manager reads.

STEP FOUR: INTERVIEWING

The interview process is probably the most action-packed experience you will face in business school. All the preparation you do comes down to a few face-to-face meetings with people you've probably never met before, and most of it happens within a few short but intense weeks.

Most firms begin the process with on-campus, first-round interviews, designed to "screen" candidates and narrow the list to a manageable number. Depending on the process at your school, students will either be selected for interviews through a lottery (in which students express an interest in the firm and the school randomly selects the list) or an auction process (in which students are given a certain number of "points" at the start of the recruiting season, with the interview spots going to those who bid the highest number of points). Alternatively, the firm may simply compile its own list of students to be interviewed based on the resumes and cover letters it has received.

Some firms will interview more students than others; it depends on their size and hiring needs. The on-campus, first-round interviews are usually only twenty or thirty minutes long and conducted by an employee at the associate or vice-president level. Usually there is only one person interviewing you at a time, although sometimes there may be two.

A small number of firms will extend offers after only one round. But most will have a number of later rounds, anywhere from one to three, which are sometimes held on-campus but are usually at the firm's corporate offices or at a local hotel. Often these "callbacks" involve all-day visits, sometimes with up to a dozen half-hour interviews in a row. The farther you go in the process, the more senior the interviewers will be; hiring decisions are usually made by partners, managing directors, or other high-ranking officers. Often, later-round interviews involve more than one person; "two-on-ones" are particularly popular with investment and commercial banks.

Not all MBA interviews are of the usual "tell-me-about-yourself" sort. Case interviews were popularized by consulting firms but have become more popular in other industries as well. In a case interview, the interviewer will pose a business problem or situation and ask you to verbally outline your approach to solving it, as well as your recommendation. As you discuss your solution, the interviewer will often interrupt and ask questions to test your analysis before permitting you to continue. Case interviews are generally intended to give the firm a chance to evaluate your thought process, your ability to think on your feet, and your poise. It is generally a good idea to ask questions of the interviewer to clarify the case before beginning your analysis, and the interviewer will usually expect you to do so.

How to Prepare

Thorough preparation is very important to your success in the MBA interviewing process. While some of your success will depend on factors that are beyond your control, such as the personality of the person interviewing you, there are a number of things you can do to stack the odds in your favor.

First, make sure you are comfortable with every word on your resume. Many recruiters like to ask in great detail about particular pieces of your background. These types of questions are great opportunities for you to shine and talk about something you really know. On the other hand, if you can't say something meaningful about your own experience, you will likely not make a good impression on the interviewer as someone who can add value to her business.

Before you begin interview season, study your own resume carefully if you haven't read it in a while.

Second, develop responses to common interview questions. There are a few things that you can be pretty sure an interviewer is going to ask, and the better you can answer these queries, the better you will do in the rest of the interview. Such typical questions include:

- Tell me about yourself.
- Why do you want this job?
- What are your strengths and weaknesses?
- What are your short- and long-term career goals?
- Why did you decide to go to business school?

While this list is by no means exhaustive, it is a good starting point for an approach to any interview.

Third, give shape to your answers and make yourself more intriguing by coming up with a "story" about yourself and your career goals. You don't have to present yourself as someone who has always known exactly what he wanted to do. But a successful interviewee puts his skills, his experiences, and his goals for the future into a believable "narrative" of sorts that makes himself sound believable and sincere. Think about what you want and what you have done, and develop a brief but compelling story about how that has driven you toward the job for which you are interviewing.

Fourth, prepare your own questions about the firm. This demonstrates to the interviewer that you have a genuine interest in the firm. Moreover, at some point in the interview the interviewer will likely give you an opportunity to ask questions, and you had better have some!

Finally, practice makes perfect. Just as an actor would never go to an opening-night performance without having rehearsed, so too should a job-seeker avoid going into interview season without feeling comfortable with his presentation. Practice answering the typical interview questions with friends or in mock interviews at your career center until you can give plausible answers with ease. If you expect a lot of case interviews, practice with your friends or other students who may have experience with them. Your school's Consulting Club or career center may also have samples on file. These steps will make you feel more relaxed and in control, and improve your chances of success.

Other tips for interviewing:

- **Research the company before going into the interview.** Companies like to make offers to people who they know are seriously interested in working for them; just as you wouldn't like to be rejected by them, they don't want to be rejected by you. Often they will probe your interest by asking you about the firm and what specifically makes you want to work for them. To prepare, read through whatever published materials you can get your hands on, whether in your career library or through on-line resources such as NEXIS or Dow Jones. The more you know about the company, the more serious you will be taken as a candidate.

- **Show enthusiasm and energy.** Along similar lines, companies like to hire people who are excited about working for them. Don't be afraid to show some enthusiasm for the job. When they ask you why you want to work for them, tell them how great they are...they have egos just like anyone else.

- **Don't be obsequious.** With that said, there is a fine line to walk between excitement and brown-nosing. Nobody likes a candidate who is overly eager to please; it makes them look desperate and weak. Present yourself as someone who knows what she wants, and if she doesn't get it from the person interviewing her now then she'll get it from someone else. There is more than one company out there that can meet your professional needs.

- **View interviewing as a two-way process.** As much as the interviewers are evaluating you, you should be evaluating the interviewers as well. Not every job is right for you, and not every company is the right fit for your personality and style. Look at your interviews as a chance for two people to get to know each other a little better to see if they can work well together.

- **Pay attention to your physical presentation.** Perhaps more important than the things you say are the way you look when you say them. Hygiene is of course important; make sure you look clean and fresh. Your clothes, too, can say a lot about the way you take care of yourself. Dress stylishly without going overboard; you want to look somewhere in between suave and simple. Finally, make sure you appear relaxed in your posture and mannerisms. Practice sitting in an open, relaxed way, and make sure you don't fidget while you talk.

- **Try to be yourself as much as possible.** While it is true that you are trying to put on a show during an interview, it is also true that a really good interviewee will let his true self show through. If you try to present yourself as someone you're not, you probably won't be very convincing and, at best, you might end up with a job that really isn't right for you. Be yourself and answer questions in a positive way, but honestly.

- **Don't let negative experiences get you down.** Most interviewers are basically nice people; they want to learn as much as they can about you so they can make an informed evaluation, but they will be respectful of your feelings and your integrity. Once in a while, however, you may meet someone whose goal is to make you feel three inches small and see how you handle it. We all know the type. If this happens, don't let it get to you. The odds are, the interviewer does this to everyone, and it's nothing personal. If it is, then you probably never stood a chance anyway; write it off as a firm you wouldn't want to work for after all, and move on. It's just an interview; it's not your life.

SUMMER INTERNSHIPS

Although most of the recruiting process described above refers to the hunt for a full-time job, there is also a small market for MBA summer interns and most of the above advice also applies to the summer job search.

Many companies use the summer between the first and second year of business school to hire MBA interns. This allows companies to evaluate prospective applicants for full-time positions at the firm. The internship also gives the company a chance to let a promising MBA student see what it would be like to work at the firm after graduation.

Most of the recruiting process for summer internships is very similar to the process for full-time employment. Generally, MBA students begin to mail resumes for summer internships in the Fall of their first year of business school, some time around November or December. Companies usually respond to these resumes in the Spring by inviting a list of students to interview for summer positions on campus or at the firm's offices.

The market for MBA interns varies widely by industry, geographic region, and business school. Generally, there is a larger market for summer interns in brand management, management consulting, investment and commercial banking, and investment management. MBAs are usually hired by the larger firms, although many students go to work for small companies in the summertime. Summer pay varies from zero for some public sector internships to $1,800 per week for some summer jobs in management consulting. The more prestigious schools tend to have more success placing their students in the higher paying internships.

Use the summer internship to learn more about yourself and your career options. If you are in a two-year program, the summer experience is a great way to explore something new and find out what else is out there. If you want to make a career switch, the summer is a great time to get a taste of a new field and put some new experience down on your resume. More importantly, a summer internship in your future industry of choice shows second-year recruiters that you are serious about the business. If you want to get into finance, for example, you are better off taking a lower paying portfolio analyst position for the summer than taking a higher paying internship unrelated to finance. Even if you know that you want to stay in the same industry you were in before B-school, you might want to think about using the summer as a chance to try something different. If you like it, you can stay; if not, you can be that much more confident in your career decision.

FINAL SUGGESTIONS

In many ways, recruiting is the most important part of business school. Although people have a wide range of personal reasons for getting an MBA—whether it be academic challenge, a new experience, or professional skill development—in the end, almost everybody wants the same thing: the best job he or she can get. "Making the most money—that's the bottom line! Who cares if we like it here or not?" explained one MBA in our survey.

And nearly everyone succeeds in the job search. Despite the criticism business schools have taken over the last few years, the fact remains that an MBA will open up amazing opportunities for you. Some of the most interesting, challenging, and lucrative jobs in the world are open only to those with graduate business degrees. For many other positions, an MBA makes you an instant candidate. "I doubled my salary with my MBA!" boasted one Purdue student. A Rice University MBA wrote, "I came here earning $35K a year and have accepted a position at $100K-plus a year already!"

Unfortunately, the recruiting process at school can be very trying, even for the strongest among us. One Stanford MBA reported that the recruiting grind "is unbelievably pressure packed, especially when classmates have offers and you don't." Everybody seems to be shooting for the same jobs with the same companies, and there just aren't enough positions with high-profile firms for everyone. Business school students are generally used to getting what they want, and chances are that they have rarely been in a situation where so many people as qualified as they are want the same things. Many are surprised by how competitive the process can be; furthermore, they get frustrated and upset when their performance does not meet their original expectations.

While everyone at business school has had a good amount of success in their lives, that doesn't mean they don't get nervous once in a while. And everybody—that's right, everybody—gets that sinking feeling in their stomach when they think about the job search. Just the idea of hundreds of ambitious, motivated, capable people scrambling to make the best impression possible to a bunch of people whom they've never met before can be enough to give just about anyone an anxiety attack.

If you get nervous, that's okay—you're certainly not alone. But what follows is some advice on the recruiting process from those who have gone through it, which should help you prepare for the road that lies ahead and avoid having to check into the school's psychological center. With the right attitude and a little bit of maturity, recruiting can be a two-way learning process that helps you understand more about yourself and your future.

Here are a few suggestions to help make your job search as pleasant and rewarding as possible.

- **Accept the fact that everyone in your class is at least as qualified as you are.** The sooner you understand this, the better off you will be. No matter how good you think your resume is, almost everyone else thinks theirs is just as good—and they are probably right. Coming out of college, it was probably good enough to impress a top local firm that you graduated cum laude and were president of your sorority. At business school, however, everyone has their strong points, and to recruiters you all look pretty much the same. If you start to think that you will have an easy time getting jobs because of your unique background, you could get complacent and be left holding the bag. Focus on your selling points, work very hard to convey them, and you will be much better off.

- **Take a broad perspective on the landscape of job opportunities.** If you hang around business schools long enough, you might come to think that the only jobs in the world worth having are in investment banking and consulting. Although these fields are clearly popular, lucrative, and accessible to MBAs, they are not the only things you can do with your life. Ask yourself these questions: How many people do I know who have successful, prosperous careers in business? How many of these people are investment bankers or consultants? Probably not very many. There's a whole universe out there. Use your time away from the rat race to explore what might be best for you.

- **Don't compare yourself to your peers.** Business school is an opportunity for you to find a challenging career that suits your interests and abilities. It is not a contest to see who can get the most prestigious job. Within the small, closely-knit communities that B-schools are, it is inevitable that people will try to measure their accomplishments against those of their classmates. While it may be tempting to want to raise people's eyebrows by taking a job with the most prestigious firm you can find, keep in mind that when you leave campus, nobody's going to be around to be impressed; you're going to have to get out of bed and actually go to work. By the same token, everyone has a unique set of skills and desires, and what's right for your best friend is probably not right for you. Don't let the perception that everyone you know seems to be going to Wall Street make you doubt your self-worth if you're not going there too.

- **Don't have your heart set on one particular job.** While it is great to be focused and know exactly what you want, it can be dangerous to limit your interests too narrowly. No matter how much it may be true that companies seem to be in an MBA-hiring frenzy, the fact remains that most firms make offers to at best one in five students whom they interview, and usually it is more like one in ten or twenty. And no matter how good you may be, there are factors such as personality and timing that are out of your control in the recruiting process. Be realistic and pursue a good number of opportunities. If you land your dream job, great; if not, you won't have missed on all the other interviews.

- **Have a "plan-B" in place.** Along similar lines, many fields are difficult to break into, especially if you are a career-changer. While it is very likely that with determination and hustle you can enter just about any industry you want, you need to have some other options available if fortune doesn't turn your way. In other words, explore more than one field on the off chance that your experience just isn't right to break into the area or industry you want at this time.

- **Don't rely on your placement office.** At most schools, much of the on-campus recruiting is packed into a few weeks early in the season. While it is true that this period offers the most concentrated window of opportunity you will probably ever see, do not fall into the trap of thinking that if you don't strike gold during on-campus recruiting your job prospects are over. "I plan to get my own job. If I had to rely on career services and the companies that come, I wouldn't be as pleased" wrote one Rochester MBA. Most corporations do not have formal MBA recruiting programs, and many do not even think about their hiring needs until a couple of months before they're ready to bring someone on board. As a result, many of the most interesting job openings come late in the school year. Don't be afraid to wait a while to accept a job and don't pin all your hopes on the on-campus recruiting season. Otherwise, you may miss some great opportunities.

  Moreover, B-school placement offices tend to vary in effectiveness. Therefore, it is important not to rely on your placement office to get a job for you. Only a small percentage (a minority at most schools) obtain their jobs through the placement office or on-campus recruiting. In addition, the placement services at many B-schools are notoriously poor. "The placement office needs work," wrote one University of Florida MBA, and another went so far as to call it "miserable." "The placement center is hopelessly bogged down in red tape," complained one MBA from the University of Colorado, where only thirty-five companies recruited on-campus in 1994. "I thought I would get some more help in my job search than I'm getting," wrote a frustrated Emory MBA. Perform an independent job search beyond the placement office to make sure that you are exploring all possibilities.

- **Keep a long-term perspective.** The job you take coming out of business school will probably be the first of a long string of jobs, and it is not imperative that you hit a home run immediately. (Chances are none of your friends will be taking their first jobs as CEOs!) View your job search as the first step down a long road, and keep it in the perspective of your long-term career plan. Recruiting does not end after business school; there will be plenty of opportunities for you to move up the ranks, even to change careers if you want. Statistics show that the average MBA has already changed jobs twice within five years of graduation!

Final Thoughts

Looking back, most MBAs agree that business school was both one of the most exhilarating and most demanding experiences of their lives. Business school is also the last time most of you will ever be students, so take full advantage of all that B-school has to offer before you re-enter the job market and the real world for good.

Although by itself an MBA is probably not going to be your Golden Passport, the MBA will go a long way to opening doors that would otherwise remain closed. Armed with an MBA, in addition to your work experience and other skills, you will surely have an edge as you pursue your goals in the years ahead.

MBA-ese

Air Hog: An MBA student who monopolizes class discussions.

Call-back: An invitation to return for a second-round job interview.

Case: The staple of most MBA programs; a description of an actual business situation, which you will be asked to "solve."

Case interview: A job interview in which the interviewer asks the student to solve a case; used mostly by management consulting firms

Cold-call: How professors force unwilling MBA students to participate in class discussion.

Core: The required courses taught in the first year of business school.

Coursepacks: The thick stacks of photocopied required readings that have largely replaced textbooks at most B-schools; (also called "bulkpacks").

Ding: A rejection letter received by a B-school job applicant.

Facebook: A directory distributed to the incoming B-school class displaying each student's photograph and employment history.

Finhead: A finance major.

Happy Hour: The weekly, B-school sponsored drinking fest; held on Thursday nights at most schools.

HP 12-C: The financial calculator of choice for most MBAs.

Mailfolder: Each student's on-campus mail slot; where you'll usually receive your graded assignments, exams, and, most importantly, invitations to recruiting presentations.

Name-tent: The name tag MBAs must display on their desks; often used by professors to compel class participation from unwilling students.

Participation Grade: The portion of your overall course grade that is based on the quality and quantity of your class participation.

Poets: MBAs with liberal arts backgrounds.

Quant Jock: An MBA who excels in quantitative analysis.

Rocket Scientists: MBAs with highly quantitative backgrounds, like engineering majors.

Section: One of several subdivided groups of MBA students who take their first year courses together; (also called a "cohort").

Sharks: Overly aggressive MBA students, especially those who place an undue emphasis on B-school grades.

Touchy-feely: An adjective used by MBAs to describe any B-school course purporting to teach "softer" management skills, such as leadership or teamwork.

About the Authors

H.S. Hamadeh and Andy Richard studied finance and entrepreneurial management at the Wharton School.

The authors welcome your comments, suggestions, and quotes about B-school life. You can contact them at rupu74a@prodigy.com.